BURDEN OF TRUTH

BURDEN OF TRUTH

A PATH TO JUSTICE FOR MY FAMILY & COMMUNITY

ROBBY CARRIER BETHEL
with
KIM MALCOLM

OAKLAND, CA

Copyright © 2024 Robby Carrier Bethel with Kim Malcolm

All rights reserved. No part of this book may be used or reproduced in any manner without written permission from the publisher except in the case of brief quotations embodied in critical articles or reviews. klmalcolm@gmail.com

Cover Design: Mary Meade and Kim Malcom
Book Design: Mary Meade

Thunderhooves Press
ISBN 978-0-9995896-3-2—First edtion

Dedicated to our courageous ancestors,

our loving families,

and the children of the future

New Iberia

Oh my lord…

Yes I told my Momma

Oh my lord… This is where I live

—LEADBELLY, FROM "NEW IBERIA"

A NOTE TO THE READER

THIS IS THE STORY OF Robby Carrier Bethel, her family, her land and a lawsuit. I met Robby when I was visiting Louisiana in one of those encounters that seem both wildly unlikely but destined to happen. While I was reading local news stories one evening, a six-year-old article came up on my computer screen. It was about the Carriers, a Black family in New Iberia, 20 miles east of where I was staying in Lafayette. The story described how, sometime early in the 20th century, oil rigs were installed on the Carrier family's farmland and then, for more than 100 years, the royalties from oil production went to local white families. The article said the drilling hadn't stopped. The Carriers were planning a lawsuit.[1]

The next morning, I found the address of the woman featured in the news article, Robby Carrier Bethel. I drove to New Iberia, wondering whether I'd be asked to tea or asked to leave. I left the highway at the first New Iberia exit and followed a straight road east through thousands of acres of post-harvest sugarcane stubs.

After a few miles, I was on the west side of New Iberia driving along rutted roads, past abandoned buildings in weedy lots, and storefronts that looked like they were on the verge of closing for good.

Just past a parking lot full of orange school buses and an abandoned self-service car wash, I pulled up in front of a small house with a screened-in porch and striped window awnings. A live oak tree shaded most of the house and a heat-seared lawn. I took a deep breath. I walked to the single step separating the front door from the front yard and knocked on the door. A heavyset Black woman appeared behind the screen door wearing a black t-shirt with white lettering that said "If you knew my family, you would understand." Her features were soft and strong. She appeared to be in her early fifties. She was the woman in the news story.

"I'm sorry to bother you," I said. "I am looking for Robby Carrier Bethel."

"Yes," she replied. "How can I help you?"

I told her I wanted to write about her family. She wanted to talk.

That fall, I got to know Robby and her family's story, usually over stir-fry lunch at the local Chinese diner. She told me about her family's plans to file a lawsuit against the people who she believed stole her family's oil, and why it had taken her family more than 100 years to do that. For a while, she was careful. I was careful too; believing that getting too close might compromise my writing, as if I were a journalist, which I was not.

After a while, we called each other "Sister," and I got to share a little part of Robby's journey with her. She talked about patience and faith and fear. She spoke in metaphors at times and sometimes made surprising connections. One time, I asked her how she felt about living on St. Jude Street. St. Jude is the patron saint of lost causes. "It's okay," she said. "My last name is Bethel and that means "House of God." This is how Robby keeps going.

The land and the City of New Iberia are an important part of Robby's story. They are cause and effect, judge and jury, angel and devil. The region is called "Acadiana" or "Cajun country." It's full of roots music and rich food, usually deep-fat fried. The land is flat, with meandering bayous, sugarcane fields, and stands of live oak. During much of the year, the weather is hot and humid, prone to hurricanes and flooding. For the last 100 years, much of the sugarcane-covered land has also served the oil industry and the businesses that support drilling.

It's hard to see what remains of the natural state of things here. The land has been farmed, paved, and polluted. The waterways are channeled, leveed, dug, dammed, drilled, and sandbagged. Except for the swamps. If you tried to take the swamps from the alligators and egrets and cedar trees, you'd probably end up with another swamp.

The City of New Iberia, where Robby lives, is tucked away from the world, six miles off the highway and in some ways a million miles from what we, as a country, tell ourselves we aspire to. Hanging on to the some of the best and some of the worst of our history, New Iberia seemed exhausted and hopeful, audacious and fearful, Black and White.

I met a white woman named Bonnie in New Iberia who expressed a lot in one short conversation. One day, we sat on the patio of her plantation-style house on the edge of town. She was probably in her mid-50's, modern, confident, and obviously educated. While her handsome hunting dogs ducked in and out of my field of vision, I told her I wanted to write about a family whose oil resources had allegedly been stolen for 100 years by oil companies and local white families. I told her I was interested in her perspective on how that could happen in New Iberia.

"Are you going to tell the other side of that story?" she asked. I wasn't expecting the question.

"I would like to," I said. "I guess that's why I'm here with you."

She paused for what seemed like a long time and then said, "Have you seen how bad the roads are in this town?"

I said I had, although I didn't understand how potholes were relevant. She didn't elaborate. Robby later told me that road repairs in New Iberia had been subsidized for many years by one of the families getting the royalties from the oil Robby believed was taken from her land.

At first, I asked myself many times why I — a white woman from California — should care about what goes on in the little town of New Iberia. At first, maybe I was making up for the mistakes I made with my adopted Black son, Gabe, who grew up in a liberal white community I wrongly believed would be colorblind. Or maybe I was looking for a way to forgive myself for the damage caused by my ancestors who enslaved Black people in the state of North Carolina. But ultimately, I cared because of Robby, who encouraged my belief that most people have a deep connection to the truth. Some, like Robby, are just better than others at living it.

Robby's story is really three connected stories — about a family, a lawsuit, and the community of New Iberia, Louisiana. Some of the connections are surprisingly obvious, but some require some very complicated understandings and assessments. There were times when something — maybe a document or a comment — cast doubt in my mind about some part of Robby's story. There may still be things that raise doubts. But in every case where I researched my doubts, what I learned would strengthen my confidence in what Robby had told me and the conclusions she reached. She never assumed anything. She knew she needed evidence.

I began this journey thinking I would write a book. Over time, I realized Robby's story isn't one that can be fairly told by an outsider. I helped with the logistics and the mechanics, but the stories and the insights are Robby's. This is Robby's truth.

…Kim Malcolm

TIME LINE

1790 – Joseph Damas Carrier, the son of a freed slave, inherits land in Opelousas Tract near Lafayette

1868 – The grandson of Joseph Damas Carrier, Louis Carrier, takes title to 23 acres of land near Little Bayou outside of New Iberia in Iberia Parish

1895 – Alphonse Carrier inherits the land at Little Bayou from his father, Louis

1916 – Alphonse Carrier Jr. is shown as a signatory to a pooling agreement with Texas Oil Company; oil is found on land adjacent to the Carrier property

1917 – Approximate date of the initiation of exploration for oil on or near the Carrier land

1936 – Date of a plate on extraction facilities found on Carrier land, identifying Texas Oil Company as owner of facilities

1944 – New Iberia welding school opens; New Iberia Black professionals run out of town by sheriff

1945 – Alphonse Carrier Jr. dies and leaves Carrier Land to his sons, Murphy and Melvin.

1954 – Document allegedly signed by Melvin Carrier (with the name "Murphy Carrier" in the signature box) grants royalties from oil on the Carrier property to Mayo Romero

1954 – Carrier house on the south side of the bayou burns down; Murphy and Melvin Carrier build new house on the north side of the bayou; fence with locked gate installed on Carrier land south of the bayou

1957 – Date of document allegedly authorizing Mayo Romero to act as agent for the Carriers in an agreement for royalties with Olin Gas Transmission Company

1970 – Date of document allegedly permitting the transfer of the Carrier property from "Charly Jones" to Glen Romero

1971 – Date of document allegedly granting royalties to the Schwing family for oil extracted on the Carrier land

1987 – Robby visits Carrier property with her father, Melvin Carrier, and finds a plaque dated 1934 with the name Texas Oil Company

1995 – Melvin Carrier dies after asking Robby to "make right" the "terrible injustice" against the Carrier family

1998 – Date of document granting Glen Romero a $60,000 "bonus" for permitting SONAT to conduct seismic exploration on the Carrier property

2003 – Robby's uncle, Murphy Carrier, dies after encouraging Robby to pursue justice for the Carrier land at Little Bayou

2005 – Robby learns her grandfather died of a pulmonary embolism

January 2006 – The Carrier attorney, Floyd Johnson, files succession petition in 16th District court with Robby as administrator

2008 – Succession petition of the Carrier family granted by 16th District court

2011 – Karen May hires attorney Craig Stewart and serves Robby papers to remove her as administrator in the succession case

January 2013 – Article in The Independent describes allegations of fraud perpetrated on the Carrier family

2012-17 – City of New Iberia eliminates funding for West End recreational programs, paves over swimming pool, closes West End library, tennis courts

July 2018 – Carrier family files lawsuit in 16th District Court with Karen May as administrator

April 2019 – Preliminary hearing in May v Romero held by Judge Sigur in the 16th District Court of Louisiana

August 2019 – Court dismisses Carrier lawsuit on the basis of "prescription," finding that the Carriers waited too long to file their lawsuit

September 2019 – Defendants of the Duhe family submit an untimely letter to the 16th District Court in opposition to the Carrier lawsuit

October 2019 – Carrier family files Notice of Appeal in 3rd Circuit Court with Robby Carrier Bethel as administrator

July 2020 – Carrier family files Appellate Brief in 3rd Circuit Court

November 2020 – Louisiana's 3rd Circuit Court affirms the lower court's dismissal of the Carrier lawsuit on the basis that the plaintiffs waited too long to file their lawsuit

CARRIER FAMILY TREE *

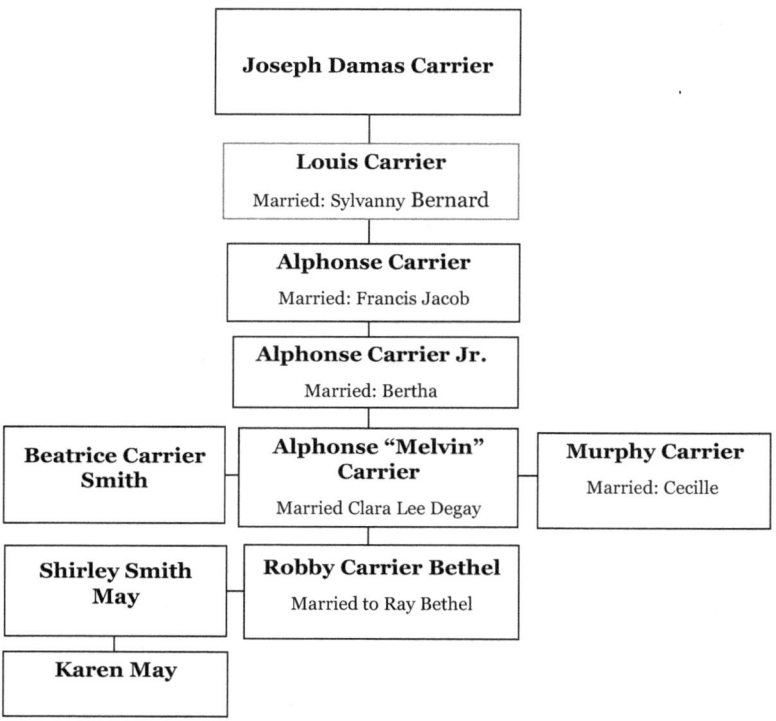

* Of those named in the narrative

PROLOGUE

Like most people, I guess, I've had moments in my life that changed me and the way I see the world. Sometimes it's something in my mind, like a revelation, and sometimes it's something that comes to me from the outside. These moments haven't all been what I'd choose for myself or the people I love, but they're the truth and I think that's the best I can hope for.

One of those moments was the day my granddaddy made it to the Third Circuit Appellate Court of the state of Louisiana. On July 27, 2020, I filed a 19-page brief on behalf of Louis Carrier and 23 acres of Louisiana farmland. It was written in a complicated way, but it really just asked for one thing: to give me a chance to make my case and show that powerful people had hurt my family for more than 100 years.

Filing that document was more important than all the work I did to get there and all the hope I had. I'd been working on that lawsuit for 20 years. It was slow because I was busy with my children and grandbabies, or working. Sometimes, things happened that were out of my control and I didn't always fight, believing things would turn around, and sometimes they did. But also, I was scared at times.

My fears slowed me down, but I always came back to it. I wanted justice for my family. I wanted powerful people to fix the damage on the land. I wanted them to admit they'd been wrong and that they'd hurt generations of my family and my community. Most of all, I wanted the truth.

CONTENTS

A Note To The Reader / ix

Time Line / xv

Prologue / xix

1: Little Bayou / 1

2: The Secrets / 5

3: The Carrier Land / 11

4: Oil / 15

5: Lake Peigneur / 19

6: Da Berry / 23

7: The Fishing Rodeo / 29

8: Clara Lee DeGay Carrier / 37

9: The School Board / 49

10: Leaving and Coming Home / 57

11: Daddy / 67

12: The City Services We Wanted / 73

13: The Check / 81

14: The Pulmonary Embolisms / 87

15 : Research / 93

16: Ghosts / 101

17: The First Lawyer / 105

18: The Second Lawyer / 113

19: The Independent / 115

20: Flood / 119

21: The Third Lawyer / 123

22vSister / 127

23: The City Services We Didn't Want / 131

24: Envision Da Berry / 139

25: The Lawsuit / 147

26: The Judgment / 157

27: The Transcript / 165

28: A Contract / 171

29: The Fourth Lawyer / 175

30: Changing the Administrator / 179

31: Getting the Files / 185

32: The Notice of Appeal / 193

33 : The Tax Assessor Again / 195

34: Legal Procedures / 201

35: The Pandemic / 207

36: Master Plan / 215

37: The Decision on Appeal / 221

38: Where Things Stand / 229

Acknowledgments / 235

Endnotes / 237

"If you surrendered to the air, you could ride it."

—TONI MORRISON

1

LITTLE BAYOU

IT WAS THE FIRST TIME I'd been to the Carrier land since I was a little girl. It was hot and humid like most September days in Louisiana. At the time, I only knew two things about the land. My grandma once lived there, and, when I was a child, my family only talked about it in whispers.

We went to the land that day because Daddy wanted me to build a house out there. I preferred to stay in town so my children would be near their friends and schools, but I told my daddy I'd go with him. I wanted to connect my memories to the real place.

My daddy and I drove out to the region called Little Bayou, several miles southeast from where we lived in New Iberia. We didn't talk much. My daddy was a quiet person and I was like him. I hung my arm out the window and let the breeze hit my face. Just past the old roadhouse, Daddy pulled off on to the narrow dirt road that defined the southern boundary of the property. The car groaned and squeaked getting over and around the potholes. We drove along a wall of sugarcane stalks that lined the road on one side, almost dry, ready for burning and then the harvest.

The land looked the same as it always had, flat and cut down the middle by Little Bayou creeping quietly behind a line of live oak and scrub.

The land looked the same, but it felt different from my memories of it. Now, it connected me to my community and generations of my family who had owned the land for more than 100 years. The land held me to the place I'd grown up.

When Daddy and I got out of the car, I could hear farm machinery off in the distance and a barking dog. The air was damp and clean. Daddy picked up a few pieces of trash on the side of the road and stuffed them into his pocket. He leaned against the car and waved his hand along the horizon to indicate the boundaries of the property.

I followed Daddy's gaze until I saw the oil derrick behind a stand of trees and shrubs. I walked toward it. Daddy was watching me. I could tell by the way his body bent in my direction that he was uneasy when I crossed the ditch toward the derrick. As I walked around the rusting metal, I saw an iron plaque at the base of the derrick and leaned over to read it.

The plaque said, "Texas Oil Company 1934."

"Leave it alone, Robby." I'd heard him say something like that several times over the years when the subject of the Carrier land came up in family conversations. Daddy was a peaceful person and, looking back, I think he was protecting me from trouble. He would change his mind about that in some of his last words to me.

2

THE SECRETS

I LEARNED AS A CHILD that the Carrier land had secrets, but I knew the Carrier land before I knew its secrets. For years it was just a flat open space covered in sugarcane where my grandma lived. My daddy stopped at the land to visit my grandma most mornings when he was driving me to kindergarten. The house was small and built of swamp cedar with a covered porch on the front. My grandma didn't have a car so she had to rely on Daddy to make sure she had enough to eat. Daddy would leave my grandma sweets or leftovers or a bag of groceries. The times I waited in the car, I could hear my daddy's voice, asking Grandma about her health and what she needed by Friday to get through the weekend.

Sometimes, I went inside with my daddy. The house was dark and usually smelled of fried food, and something like perfume. In the winters, my grandma would be on the old blue couch, wound inside heavy blankets like a baby. In the summers, Grandma would be on the old blue couch, fanning herself with a worn-out magazine. Grandma would always tell me, "Robby, what a beauty you are!" That made me feel beautiful. Feeling beautiful was how I felt on the Carrier land.

After I started the first grade, I didn't go to my grandma's with my daddy in the mornings. My school was close to home, so I walked there and then my grandma died that year.

But over time, I learned more about the Carrier land. Some members of my family shared half-finished stories in whispers at family gatherings, like Thanksgiving or Christmas or reunions with aunties and uncles. After eating and maybe a little drinking, someone would move the conversation from Christmas gifts and recipes and memories, to something about the Carrier land. The stories were never clear or complete, but I sensed mystery and fear because these conversations ended quickly after a lot of shushing.

Two of my aunties were bolder than the old people who were raised to be quiet and scared. The aunties were the most likely to start those conversations. They lived with the secrets every day because they cooked and cleaned for some of New Iberia's white families. Aunt Eyola worked for Dr. LeBourgeois until she died. She lived in our neighborhood, but we didn't see her much on the holidays until the evenings. She didn't have any children so she worked on holidays serving the Le

Bourgeois family dinners and cleaning up. She made cookies and candies for the holidays weeks ahead of time and we loved going to her house because she'd have goodies set out for us.

Aunt Eyola was always dressed in a white work outfit when we saw her because she worked so many hours. She had a nice house in the West End that she'd bought from her work for white families in Beaumont, Texas. At the time, Blacks couldn't stay in New Iberia hotels, so she rented out the extra rooms in her house for a few dollars a night to people who were in town looking for work, and men who wanted a place for a rendezvous. Aunt Eyola had a black bird named Bill. When my aunt had boarders, she'd put a sheet over Bill's cage so he couldn't see who was there.

Aunt Eyola was smart about the wealthy white families in town. Sometimes, Mrs. LeBourgeois gave Aunt Eyola some used china as gifts. She made a point to tell me the china sets were never whole place settings, as if it were a message about what they thought of her. She once told me Dr. LeBougeois was one of the people who tried to steal our land.

She didn't keep money in the bank because the Duhes and the Schwings owned shares of the banks in town. She thought they were thieves too, so she hid her savings in her house. She always had dollar bills for us when we visited.

Aunt Rachel lived in our neighborhood and she'd also bought her own house from saving her earnings when she was in Beaumont, Texas. She was the best Avon seller in the community. She was well-dressed and pretty, and she kept track of everyone's birthday. One time she told the story of my father's birth. His name was supposed to be Melvin but the midwives thought his momma said "Melgun," so that's what they wrote on his birth certificate. When he was growing up, my daddy thought his name was Melvin. He didn't find out his legal name was Alphonse Melgun until he was 62 when he applied for Social Security.

Aunt Rachel once tried to put together the family tree, but that turned out to be difficult because of how hard it was to find records of Black families here. Aunt Rachel was the first person who told me if you don't have government records, you can't prove who you're related to or what you own. She worked for the Bernards cleaning and cooking. Ms. Bernard was part of the Schwing family. Aunt Rachel told me the Bernards were paying her from the money the Schwings were getting from our land.

In her last days, I drove Aunt Rachel to a nursing home. She seemed to know it was going to be one of her last car rides because she wanted to drive by the Carrier land on the way. She wanted to see the place where she was born and grew up. We stopped at the special live oak where the children's heights had been marked on the bark as they were growing up. That was a Monday. On Tuesday, I had lunch with Aunt Rachel at the nursing home. She died that night.

Those family gatherings taught me ways to learn the truth behind the secrets. Because of the whispers and the shushing, I learned to ask questions around the edges of things. Because no one ever shared more than a sentence or two, I learned to piece together things I'd heard at different times. After I started investigating the Carrier land, I learned that, if I let them, the voices would speak to me a second time.

3

THE CARRIER LAND

What I know about the Carrier land begins with my great-great granddaddy, Joseph Damas Carrier, who was called Damas. Damas' mother didn't name him. Damas was originally given the name Joseph Carrier by the man who enslaved him, who was also named Joseph Carrier. As an adult, Damas didn't go by Joseph because he didn't want to share the name of the man who enslaved him. Damas Carrier was the first in what is called the "Black Line," that is, the first of the Carrier family who was Black.

Damas lived on Joseph Carrier's sugarcane plantation in a region called Opelousas District in the state of Louisiana. You might have heard of Opelousas. In 1868, southern Democrats massacred 200 Black residents in Opelousas because they voted in local Republicans who supported civil rights. This was supposed to discourage Blacks from voting in future elections.

But before the Civil War and the Opelousas Massacre, Damas probably lived like most enslaved Black men in Louisiana, working long and hard in the sugarcane fields. Damas probably worked the sugarcane without any hope his life would ever change. But Joseph Carrier, the man who enslaved Damas, was also his father and so there was hope. Joseph Carrier believed his white sons — Damas' half-brothers — would keep Damas in slavery if they inherited him. Joseph Carrier wanted Damas to be freed. That might seem kind but, under the circumstances, it was probably about as kind as putting someone closer to the starting line after breaking his leg.

After Joseph Carrier died, Bailey gave Damas his papers of manumission, proving Damas was a free man. Joseph Carrier owned a lot of land, and in his will, he left Damas something like 20 acres. In the years that followed, Damas worked the land in sugarcane until he made enough money to buy his mother's freedom. To free her, Damas attended a court hearing in front of a judge. Blacks didn't normally have access to the courts in those days so we don't know exactly how that happened. The judge asked Damas why a son would want to free his enslaved mother, expressing a concern that Damas might sell his enslaved mother into slavery a second time. Apparently, Damas was convincing, because the judge approved his petition. Damas paid the value of his mother and freed her.[2]

We don't know more than that. I couldn't find any records of what happened to the land Damas inherited from Joseph Carrier, but it was probably somehow stolen from him. Here in New Iberia, many Black families once owned farm land given to them by the federal government after the Civil War. Local residents have stories about how their families were swindled out of the family's land. Something I didn't learn in school, and I doubt that many did, is that a lot of this happened after Rutherford B. Hayes became president in 1877. After the Civil War, the federal government tried to protect freed slaves during Reconstruction. Hayes ended all that as part of a deal he struck after losing the presidential election to Samuel Tilden. Even though Hayes lost the popular vote and the Electoral College vote, he promised politicians in the Southern States he'd stop enforcing federal laws protecting Black citizens if they would submit electoral college votes in Hayes' favor. And they did.

When he became president, Hayes kept his promise and ended federal oversight. That gave the state of Louisiana the freedom to pass Jim Crow laws, making racial discrimination legal. It also gave white individuals a lot of freedom to steal from Blacks and deny legal protections. And they did that, often with the help of government officials. Tax collectors worked with developers or the local court to permit a fraudulent sale, sometimes without the knowledge of its owner. Historically, and even today, Black landowners couldn't fight to keep their land or recover it. Lawyers representing Black clients against whites were hard to find. Blacks who objected could expect trouble.[3]

Although my family doesn't know what happened to the Carrier land in Opelousas Land District, we know a lot about another piece of land. In 1868, the United States Government granted 23 acres of land to Damas' grandson, Louis, as payment for serving in the Union Army. The land was in Iberia Parish 20 miles east. It was swampy and prone to flooding, but Louis Carrier and his family lived pretty well on that land. They raised cattle and horses, grew sugarcane and vegetables, and hunted game. Little Bayou ran through the land and provided a steady source of water.[4]

Louis died in 1895, leaving the land to his son, Alphonse. When Alphonse died, the land went to his son, Alphonse Jr., my granddaddy.

Just after the turn of the century when Alphonse Jr. was farming the Carrier land, a whole lot changed in Louisiana. By 1915, oil companies were discovering oil resources all over the state. Local newspapers called it the beginning of an economic renaissance.[5]

It wasn't going to be a renaissance for my family.

4

OIL

By the time my granddaddy, Alphonse Jr., was an adult, the world was addicted to petroleum, and Louisiana was in the middle of that. After World War I, oil companies descended on Louisiana. It seemed there was oil everywhere in Louisiana and, in fact, oil and gas companies would eventually be operating in every one of Louisiana's 69 parishes.[6]

My granddaddy had heard about the oil being discovered on parish properties. He knew his land sat on one of Louisiana's salt domes, which often sit on top of large deposits of oil and gas. Alphonse had heard oil men were investigating the land around his property. I later found a document in the courthouse files called a "pooling agreement." The agreement, signed in 1916 by Texas Oil Company, provided that the Carriers and several other neighboring farmers would get royalties from any oil extracted from the land sitting on the salt dome. My granddaddy never signed the document and he probably never knew about it. But his name was on it.

After that, oil rigs were installed on neighboring farms. And then, without my family's permission, oil drilling facilities were installed on the Carrier land behind a stand of live oaks and scrub near the Carrier farmhouse.

Someone from the oil company told my granddaddy that the family would be notified if oil was found on the Carrier land. The family never received any notification, but my granddaddy knew that barges going down the bayou in the middle of the night were hauling oil from his family's land. Later, my granddaddy told my daddy not to tell anyone because of what might happen if he did.

According to my daddy, at around the same time, a farmer who lived at Little Bayou, Mayo Romero, began planting sugarcane on some of the Carrier land as if the land belonged to him. He hired my granddaddy to cut the sugarcane, taking the profits from the farming operation and paying my granddaddy pennies a day for his hard labor and the labor of his sons, my Uncle Murphy and my daddy. What other choice did they have? My granddaddy couldn't use the court system to stop Romero's use of the Carrier land and he had to feed his family. In a way, he became enslaved.

My granddaddy died in 1945, leaving the Carrier land to Uncle Murphy, my daddy, and my grandma. My grandma and my daddy were still living in the house on the south side of Little Bayou where Uncle Murphy and my daddy grew up. Then, in 1954, someone lit the house on fire in the middle of the night. The Baptist church adjacent to the Carrier land was burned down a few days later, along with the birth and death records of many Blacks in the parish.[7]

The family survived the house fire, but Uncle Murphy and my daddy were advised not to return to that part of the property. No one seems to know who gave the advice, but it didn't matter. Uncle Murphy and my daddy were young men by that time and built another house away from the drilling rigs on the north side of the bayou. After that, someone installed a fence with a locked gate around the Carrier property on the south side of the bayou, where the oil rigs were located. Uncle Murphy and my daddy couldn't farm the south half of their land because of the fence and the locked gate. They couldn't farm the north half of the Carrier land because Mayo Romero was farming it.

Uncle Murphy was married by then and living in Loreauville with his wife, Cecille. Because the Carriers couldn't farm any of their 23 acres, my daddy moved off the land too. He moved to New Iberia, several miles west of the Carrier land after the house burned down. He got married to my momma, Clara Lee DeGay, and they had seven children. All along, he knew the oil company was still taking the oil from Carrier land down Little Bayou on barges in the middle of the night. He knew he couldn't object. If he hadn't been convinced of that before, the fire made it clear.

5

LAKE PEIGNEUR

IN LOUISIANA, NOTHING THAT HAPPENS involving the oil industry surprises us unless it's something that's good for regular people. The oil and gas companies have always been very powerful in Louisiana and no one ever denied it. Louisiana is full of one of the world's most valuable natural resources, and yet the people of Louisiana are some of the poorest people in America and our land is the most polluted. We all have stories about how oil companies have hurt our communities. One of those stories is about something that happened right in New Iberia's back yard at Lake Peigneur.

When I was a child, Lake Peigneur was ten feet deep and covered 1300 acres. It was a freshwater lake, nothing special but people depended on it for their living, mostly shrimpers and fishermen. Several thousand people lived around the lake. On one of its shores, a man named J.L. Bayless owned a large formal garden and an elegant mansion.

The lake sat on top of a giant salt dome. Under the lake was the Jefferson Island salt mine. Diamond Crystal Salt Mining Company had mined salt there since 1919. Because salt domes in Louisiana are usually sitting on top of oil and gas resources, a large oil rig had been installed on one side of the lake, owned and operated by Texaco.

On November 20, 1980, that oil rig drilled a hole into the salt mine below the lake, pulling billions of gallons of water into the mine below, along with barges, boats, trailer houses, the oil drilling rig, and 65 acres of land. The vortex created geysers as high as 400 feet and a 150-foot waterfall. For two days, water from a local canal was sucked into the lake until it finally filled the salt mine. After that, Lake Peigneur was 1300 feet deep and filled with salt water.

Somehow, no one died during this disaster but the natural environment around the lake was destroyed by the salt in the lake's water. Three hundred salt miners lost their jobs. Texaco admitted the accident resulted from the engineering errors of its subcontractor and paid Diamond Crystal $32 million in damages. It also paid more than $12 million to J.L. Bayless. The salt miners, however, were never compensated for losing their livelihoods. I never heard whether the 4,000 residents along the lake were ever compensated.[8]

The State of Louisiana never fined Texaco for the damage it caused to the local economy and the environment, or required Texaco to rehabilitate the land either. In fact, Louisiana's Attorney General made a public fuss about the settlement between Diamond Crystal and Texaco, foolishly disclosing that the state's liability could have exceeded $200 million.[9]

That wasn't the end of it. Several years later, the State permitted an oil and gas company, AGL Resources, to use the caverns below Lake Peigneur to store natural gas. Since then, local residents have reported giant gas bubbles on the lake's surface which, AGL assures them, aren't related to its gas operations under the lake. No one has explained what else they could be related to.[10]

6

DA BERRY

You can't really understand the story of the Carrier land without understanding where I live, New Iberia. The city's nickname is "Da Berry," a shortened version of the official name, although no one seems to know how it came about.

I have always loved my home and my neighborhood, but I learned as I grew up that New Iberia is two different places for two different kinds of people. In New Iberia, like so many other southern towns, the railroad tracks cut the city almost exactly in half. On the one side of the tracks, there are nice neighborhoods along the bayou and an old-fashioned downtown with parks and historic buildings. At the south end of downtown, there's a plantation house called "Shadows on the Teche" surrounded by live oaks and a picket fence. Downtown is nothing fancy, but it's cute and has some nice cafes and small office buildings, a museum, and an Art Deco theater. It has a dock on the bayou and a walking path and nice parks.[11]

The 40% of us who are Black mostly live on the other side in a neighborhood called the West End. Most of us struggle to get by. A lot of the buildings in the West End are in terrible shape, some abandoned, and we don't really have much here in the way of business. There are a few salons and cafes, a convenience store, and some odds and ends. The fried chicken place is near the tracks on the north side of town. It seems like all the small towns here have a fried chicken place near the train tracks. For healthier and more affordable food, because the bus service in the West End isn't convenient. There's a wonderful organic market in a renovated garage on Hopkins Street, and we want to support it, but some of the food is too expensive for most of us.

These days, we think of the train tracks as something dangerous. They criss-cross the poorest parts of town, some cutting across roads without any warning signals or gates.

It wasn't always like this. The West End used to have a lot of successful small businesses, everything you needed to be a self-reliant community, including professionals like doctors and dentists and insurance companies. After Jim Crow, the city leaders ran them out of town on a rail, literally told them to get the next train out or suffer the consequences.[12]

For a while, the train tracks brought a lot of life to the West End. A passenger train used to come through on its way to or from New Orleans, and musicians would get off the train and jam at Leo's Rendezvous, a roadhouse next to the tracks. The musicians couldn't stay in the hotels in town, so they stayed in a big old house by the tracks for a few dollars a night. When the musicians came, some of the West End people would go hear the music. As a child, I wasn't allowed to attend these jam sessions. I suspect there were some things going on that weren't very wholesome for children. But I can remember the excitement of our neighbors going from door to door to share the news that there would be music that night. A lot of famous people played at Leo's Rendezvous, including Count Basie, Otis Redding, Ray Charles, and Fats Domino.

The passenger train doesn't come through New Iberia anymore and Leo's Roadhouse sat empty for a long time before it burned down a few years ago. There isn't much music here anymore either. We still have Cajun and zydeco and blues, but mostly you have to drive out of town to hear it.

Since the passenger train stopped coming, we don't get many strangers in town. A few years ago, the mayor said he wanted to increase tourism and proposed livening up downtown but really, New Iberia feels like it's hiding from the rest of the world in a giant sugarcane field. We call these flat and fertile farmlands The Plains. Tourists stop at the Tabasco sauce plant on the other side of the highway because it has a nice restaurant and park and a place to watch the Tabasco sauce being made, but not many make it all the way into town.

New Iberia is about six miles east of the highway connecting New Orleans to places north of Lafayette. Along the highway are a few modern low-lying office buildings and a lot more metal-clad buildings that are probably businesses serving the oil and gas industry. We have valve companies, tool companies, pump companies, drill companies, hauling companies, and welding companies.

But if you ask someone here for directions, the answer will probably include a reference to a Walmart, a Home Depot, or a McDonald's. They are like a front door to many of the small towns along the highway. Generally, the buildings of large corporate businesses are a lot nicer than the ones housing businesses owned by Louisiana residents. Small local businesses don't do too well here, and it seems Acadiana is being slowly but surely overtaken.

Even overtaken, though, it's still Louisiana, different from every other state in the union. More French than English, more Catholic than Protestant, more gumbo and boudin than burgers and hot dogs. New Iberia was first settled in 1779 by a group of Spaniards, but family names here are as likely to be Broussard, Thibodeaux, or LeBlanc as Romero or Lopez. The French occupied most of Louisiana in the 18th century and a lot of French Canadians migrated here.[13]

The immigrants from Canada are what you might call our dominant culture. They were originally called "Acadian" eventually also shortened to "Cajun." For a long time, Acadian children weren't allowed to speak French or admit their family roots. The state changed its mind about this sometime in the 1980s, and there was a revival of French Canadian culture, like the food and Cajun music. You can hear the Louisiana version of French here on the radio and in songs. The Legislature also officially pronounced this part of the state "Acadiana," although less than ten percent of us are Acadian. We're mostly not-Acadian whites, not-Acadian Blacks, and a handful of not-Acadian others. So we know who's in charge.

Pretty much everyone in New Iberia is descended from immigrants and not many have moved here in the past 100 years. White or Black, most of the families in New Iberia have been here for many generations. And that creates a powerful force for maintaining the status quo.

This is just a small part of the story of New Iberia that would make a difference in the story of my family and the Carrier land.

7

THE FISHING RODEO

In a way, my life is either before or after the Fishing Rodeo. Before the Fishing Rodeo, I didn't understand that living in New Iberia in the 1960s presented some special conditions for people like me and my family. My momma, Clara DeGay Carrier, always tried to protect her seven children from feeling different or lesser in our everyday lives. She took us to the library in the white neighborhood because it had air conditioning and better books. She shopped at the supermarket in the white neighborhood where the food was better and cheaper.

Our family doctor had two waiting areas for his patients. One had nice carpeting, nice magazines on a table, and a box of toys. The other was a dark, narrow hallway with wooden folding chairs. That waiting area was hot in summer and cold in winter. A rickety plywood door faced out to the alley along St. Peters Avenue. I didn't know about the dark waiting room until my high school boyfriend told me about it years later. I never saw it because my momma took us through the front door, into the nice waiting room with the magazines and toys, and cheerful upholstered chairs. When the receptionist saw us, she would smile but she didn't wait for us to sit down. She sent us right on through to an examining room. I'm guessing we were the only family in America that didn't have to wait to be called into a doctor's office.

Momma walked us through downtown New Iberia too, and when she did, white heads turned. I thought people looked at us because my momma was so beautiful and proud. She always had her hair done nicely and walked like she knew where she was going. I was proud of my momma and my family.

My feelings of pride got complicated after the Fishing Rodeo. If you're not from Louisiana, you might not know what a fishing rodeo is. You might picture a fishing rodeo as something with horses or you might picture fish doing things horses would do. But no, in Louisiana fishing rodeos are festivals with fishing contests, and music and food. This part of Louisiana loves to celebrate with music and food. Cajun and zydeco, etouffee and oysters, shrimp gumbo and crawfish.

In those days, the Fishing Rodeo about 50 miles north in the City of Washington drew people from all over the state and probably some from Texas. I don't think there's a fishing rodeo in Washington any more. These days, you'd have to go to Grand Isle or Lake Charles for that. But when I was growing up, my daddy went to the Washington Fishing Rodeo every year. Even though the Fishing Rodeo wasn't for Blacks, Daddy always got to go because some people in the white community thought of my family as different from our Black neighbors, so my daddy's boss gave him tickets.

That year when I was seven, my daddy worked in the catfish booth. The rest of us stayed home because the Fishing Rodeo was a time for Daddy to be taking a break with his friends and drinking beer while they were frying fish and plating it up with coleslaw and french fries. That year, my daddy bought a raffle ticket for some kind of fundraiser because that's what you do to support your friends. Daddy didn't stay around for the drawing. Maybe he didn't expect to have his number called. Looking back, I suspect he didn't think about it at all because he'd had a few beers.

Anyway, that evening, Daddy arrived home from the Fishing Rodeo and he was drunk. We all knew that because he tiptoed from the front door to the couch, hoping my momma wouldn't notice. He was sweating and staring into space there on the couch when Momma shooed him off and told him to clean up before supper.

My daddy almost always followed my momma's instructions after he'd been out drinking—you know, to keep the peace. So that night he did as he was told, lurching out of his seat on the couch without comment.

I watched him make his way to the bathroom through the kitchen, where he paused to empty his pants pockets into a little garbage can. When he came back, he went out on the front porch to avoid more of Momma until we all sat down at the table.

Later, when we were eating supper, the phone rang. The phone was screwed to the wall in the hallway. This was before cellphones and the hall phone didn't move around, so my brother Marcus left the table to answer it. Marcus was older than me by a couple of years so he was allowed to answer the phone.

He listened for a minute, politely like he didn't know the person he was talking to.

Momma asked who was on the phone. Marcus put his hand over the receiver and whispered but loudly, "Somebody says Daddy won something." Momma took the phone from Marcus and asked if she could help and then she listened for a minute.

"Mello, "Momma said from the hall. She always called my daddy "Mello." "They got somebody on the phone saying you won some kind of camping equipment in a raffle. Where's your raffle ticket?"

Daddy said he thought he'd thrown it away. I guess he didn't remember emptying his pants pockets into the little garbage can in the kitchen, but I did. While Momma was still on the phone, Marcus and I went through the garbage can and found a small yellow ticket bunched up with a receipt and a used napkin. We gave the yellow ticket to Momma and she read the numbers on it to the person on the phone.

After Momma hung up the phone, she said in a loud voice to get Daddy's attention, "Mello, they say those were the winning numbers."

"Degay, leave them people with their stuff alone." My daddy always called her DeGay. "We don't need a pup tent or sleeping bags." Daddy said he didn't really care about camping equipment, especially at that time after drinking a lot of beer.

When Momma got off the phone, she took up with him again. "Mello, you need to get your ticket stub and get yourself down to Washington to collect your prize."

And of course, he did. The next day, Daddy took the ticket stub and went to Washington to redeem his prize. Momma went with him just to make sure. That afternoon, they pulled up to the front of our house with the "camping equipment." Attached to our station wagon was a brand-new camper trailer, white with a horizontal brown stripe down the center. It had louvered windows with screens, a kitchen, a sofa, beds for six people and a little table inside. Daddy was beaming when he got out of the station wagon. Some of our neighbors came to see the camper trailer, thinking the Carrier family had become somehow rich. No one had anything like it in the West End.

That camper trailer changed our summer. Instead of driving straight through to our grandma's house in Port Arthur, Texas, as we usually did, we traveled slowly and proudly across southern Louisiana to Texas. My daddy was wearing a pair of blue plaid shorts and a cowboy hat. Momma was wearing beige shorts and tennis shoes and a green sleeveless blouse. I'd never seen my parents dress like that.

It was all so exciting, being in that shiny new camper and having an adventure. We'd never been able to stay in hotels in the South, and at the time it wouldn't have mattered if we could have afforded them. So now we could sleep on the road. First, we went to Busch Gardens. We saw how they made beer in a little museum and they had animals, almost like a zoo. I'd never been to a zoo before. My brothers loved being around the animals. They petted the goats and fed them dried corn. I just watched. Although I love animals now, I was afraid of them as a child because I'd never been around them.

One night, we stayed at a KOA campground outside of Houston, Texas. When we arrived at that campground, my brothers and I were thrilled. The campground had nice bathrooms and playground equipment and a swimming pool. After the long hot drive through southern Texas, we couldn't wait to get wet. We put on our bathing suits and Momma took us down to the swimming pool. We jumped in, bobbing up and down in the clear water with a dozen other children. We waved at my mom sitting on a bench a few feet away.

Then something happened I didn't expect. One by one, the women sitting on other benches called to their children, and motioned for them to get out of the pool. A few minutes later, they were all gone. Only my brothers and I were left in the pool.

My momma didn't move or say anything. She just kept watching us in the pool as if nothing was wrong. But I knew those children had to get out of the pool because of something about us. I was hurt because those kids didn't want to play with us. I didn't know why. And I don't know how I knew, but I felt like that day was the end of my childhood.

After the Fishing Rodeo, my skin was going to define me in every part of my life and usually not in ways I'd like. But I didn't fight. As time passed, I just accepted my place in my community. When the Black kids were given the old books and the white kids got new books, I didn't think of it as an injustice. I just wanted a pretty new book like the other kids.

I avoided the pain by accepting things. My momma avoided the pain by fighting.

8

CLARA LEE DEGAY CARRIER

I WAS IN HIGH SCHOOL before I realized my momma was not normal in New Iberia. Most West End women were proud, but they stayed away from trouble. My momma fought for what she believed and she didn't pick her battles. Making a fuss about a small thing was putting the world on notice that she was paying attention to the bigger things.

Momma had a good childhood. She was raised by her dad, Clarence, and his wife, Miss Kate, Momma's step-Momma. She was an only child. Momma was raised on Weeks Island where the salt mine is. Clarence was the first Black supervisor at the salt mine and he did well at that job. He died when Momma was about five. I don't know how Miss Kate made ends meet, but my mom always loved her and Miss Kate lived with us after she got old.

Momma graduated from high school in 1956. By then, she was already acknowledged as a leader. She was president of the student body, outspoken, and a straight A student. Dr. Henderson, her principal, used to say she'd be a lawyer because of the way she thought and spoke. After she graduated, she went to Dillard University but dropped out after she married my daddy. She worked at Derlounes Cleaners. She walked two miles to work because she couldn't drive and then she was on her feet all day long, washing and ironing, while she was raising seven kids.

All that work didn't get in the way of her passion, which was justice. She was active in the NAACP and the civil rights marches. She was a fighter for her own kids as well. One of those times was my first month in high school.

I was a good student and behaved myself and I had friends, so I started high school feeling confident. I think a lot of my feelings of confidence had to do with the schools I attended as a younger child. I grew up going to segregated schools. We didn't have a lot of what the white schools had, but what we did have was a sense of community. We knew our teachers cared about us. They were nurturing and they didn't treat us differently or lesser because of our skin color. After New Iberia schools were integrated, all of that changed.

In the first week of high school, I could sense feelings of hostility and they immediately blew up into something bigger. The school had some temporary classrooms on a military base a few miles from campus. Buses would take us there for some of our classes and then bring us back at the end of the day. One day, just before the bus was about to pull out of the parking lot to head back to the main campus, a white student named Ronald got on the bus. When he saw there were no empty seats, he pointed at one of the Black girls, his way of telling her to move out of her seat so he could sit down. When she didn't get up, he touched her shoulder. She sat quietly. A couple of the Black students objected to what he was doing. Ronald responded by calling them "a bunch of niggers."

When we arrived back at campus, the boys started fighting, whites against Blacks. The police came and the other students were directed to go home. The next day, the Black boys involved in the fight were expelled from the school for the rest of the year. We heard the white boys were suspended for three days, but we saw them at school every day.

This created a lot of tension between the students and even with our teachers. I set my mind to ignore it, as I usually did, so I could focus on what I wanted. One of the things I wanted was to be a cheerleader. I loved football. I was fit and I knew I could learn the routines after a year in middle school as a song girl.

A few weeks into the school year, we were sitting in our classrooms when the school secretary announced over the loudspeaker that cheerleader tryouts were going to be on the upcoming Friday. For the girls like me who didn't know about the date in advance, there would be almost no time to practice the routines. I knew the white families had the date of the tryouts long before the announcement. I knew that most of the cheerleaders came from the town's most affluent white families and many had grown up taking dance lessons, giving them skills that would give them a great advantage in the cheerleader tryouts. But I was determined to be a cheerleader.

Later that day after the announcement, I went to the front office to get an application for the tryouts. The office assistant looked at me over her reading glasses. She didn't say anything when I asked for an application and then tossed one at me without saying anything.

I had almost no time to practice for the tryouts but I'd learned a cheer by watching TV. It went, "Two bits, four bits, a dollar. All for the Jackets, stand up and holler." On the night before the tryouts, my mom cleaned my dirty tennis shoes and covered them in white shoe polish. I wore a pair of pink shorts that my sister Glennda made me, and a white t-shirt.

On the day of the tryouts, I was ready, but I was nervous. I worked my nervousness into a feeling of anticipation while I waited my turn. As insurance, I asked Jesus to help me do my best.

The tryouts were in the boys' gym. There was no air conditioning in the gym at the time, so it was hot. About 30 girls were competing for twelve spots. There were five judges. Three were teachers and two were from the community. The previous year's cheerleaders were there too. No one else was permitted in the gym during the tryouts.

My turn was last. I thought this was supposed to be a discouraging message, but it probably worked in my favor. I watched the girls before me. They had such precise moves and enthusiasm, and I put it in my head that I would adopt their way of moving. I was almost exhausted by the time it was my turn but, as the routine began and I was moving, I felt determined and focused. The adrenaline was pumping through me and kept my movements free and flowing. I smiled and made eye contact with the judges. I could hear my voice yelling the cheers as if it belonged to someone else, loud and clear. By the end of my routine, my skin and hair were dripping with sweat. I was still nervous, but I felt powerful.

As soon as I was finished, the judges began whispering to each other. The judges asked us to wait while they tallied the scores and then they would announce the girls who would be on the team.

Just a few minutes later, they read 12 names. Mine wasn't one of them. I wanted to cry because I knew I was good enough for the team, and better than some of the ones who made it. But there was nothing I could do about it. I thanked Jesus for this experience, and I told myself I would have more time for studying and friends.

After school that day, I was working on my homework at the dining table. My homework was usually easy enough that I could get it done and still be a part of what was going on in the front of the house. Momma was unpacking a bag of groceries. In her loud voice from the kitchen, she asked about my cheerleading tryouts.

"Fine," I said, "I think I did well, Momma, but I didn't make the team." She didn't push me for details as she normally would. I knew she was tired. At the time, she was still working at the dry cleaners downtown.

The phone rang and Momma left her work putting away groceries to answer it. At first, I wasn't paying much attention, but I could feel my momma's anger rising while she was listening to someone on the other end of the line. She was breathing hard and pacing.

"Well, thank you. I will take care of this first thing in the morning." She spoke in a low voice and she was facing the refrigerator, but I heard every word she said. "Yes, I will, but I will try to keep you out of this. You have a nice evening." She hung up the phone.

I couldn't tell who was on the phone or exactly what was upsetting her, except I knew it was about the tryouts because I heard her say "Robby made it home just fine."

I knew my momma well enough to know I shouldn't ask what the call had to do with me, at least not yet. I also knew Momma was not likely to wait until morning to take care of "this."

Momma got back on the phone with Angela Johnson, the mother of the Black girl who'd been a cheerleader the year before. I could hear her asking Angela's mom about how the tryouts went. She knew Angela had been there in the gym.

I went to school that day on the bus as I usually did. Later that morning, I was called out of class to go to the principal's office. I wasn't the kind of girl who was ever called to the principal's office for causing trouble, so I was confused. When I arrived, my momma was there. We didn't speak. She looked serious. I knew she'd had to take time off from work to be there and she didn't have benefits like vacation pay, so I knew this was something important.

The secretary walked us to the inner office where the principal was sitting at a big round desk. Mr. Smith. He was chubby and authoritative, as if being polite and friendly might cause a problem. I remember thinking there was no good way to enter that room. Smiling might seem too friendly, but I didn't want to appear afraid either. I took a deep breath. When the door closed behind us, the room smelled stuffy and mildewy. Before anyone spoke, the principal called Ernie Lancon, the head of the athletic department and asked him to join the meeting.

Mr. Smith and my mom started talking without any of the usual pleasantries you might expect, like "How are you?"" or "Thank you for coming." My momma started by saying what happened to me at the tryouts wasn't fair. She said she knew something was wrong while she was waving a piece of paper in her hand. Somehow my momma had gotten the score sheet from the tryouts. She showed Mr. Smith how I'd gotten enough points to get a spot on the team. My score was higher than Jane's, who'd been picked for the team. On the score sheet, someone had scratched out my score and given some of my points to Jane. Momma didn't stop talking until she got to the point where she threatened to bring the issue to the NAACP. At the time, the NAACP was powerful in our community.

Mr. Smith replied he was going to look into it. He was fiddling with his pencil and his voice was getting deeper, going into that "how dare you" mode we heard all the time. This was not going to be an effective strategy with my momma. Mr. Smith told my Momma there had never been a problem with scoring in the past.

"A lot of the girls are disappointed when they don't get on the team, but they're always welcome to try again the next year. "

My momma sat up straighter. "No sir, we're going to fix this right now."

Mr. Smith called the secretary to come into the office and he told her to call Ms. Whittaker, to get this "straight." When the secretary came back into Mr. Smith's office, she said "they" recalculated the score and there was a mistake. Momma asked him to apologize, and he did. Imagine that.

I walked out of the office feeling the strangest combination of bewildered and happy. Something didn't feel right. Adding my name to the team like this was going to create questions in the minds of anyone who had been paying attention. I didn't want them to think this was handed to me because my momma had come to school raising hell. I wanted them to know that I made the team, but I couldn't tell anyone that. I didn't want to be noticed that way. I wanted to be noticed as the other girls had.

The first cheerleader practice was after school on the same day. I went and Jane was there. She was on the team as an "alternate."

That fall, I worked hard and I got good at the routines. I wanted to be a part of the team, but I knew I never quite belonged. The girls were mostly nice to me, but they had something with each other that made me feel alone.

Sometimes I actually was alone, not by choice, and once I was punished for it. During the school year, the cheerleaders were assigned to decorate the football locker room before every game. The girls were assigned in pairs, but the other girls helped the pairs assigned to each game. Even Jane had a partner. The signs and banners they made were artistic, made with brightly colored paints and glitter.

When it was my turn to decorate campus for a home game, I wasn't assigned to work with another cheerleader and none of the girls offered to help me. I felt a kind of shame that I was working alone, but I did the best I could. My decorations didn't look so good, as you might expect. I wasn't artistic and I couldn't afford to buy paint and the other supplies I needed to do a really good job. When the other cheerleaders saw my decorations, they were upset, so I was suspended from the team for that game. I tried so hard and I felt shame about it, like I'd failed.

Later in the school year, I was assigned to decorate the locker room a second time. One of the white cheerleaders named Jamie offered to help me. We made the banners and signs, and things turned out a little better. I was grateful for Jamie's help but it didn't feel like friendship. It felt like pity, and I didn't want pity. I wanted to work with the other girls because that's how the team worked. I wanted to be a part of that.

I kept telling myself how lucky I was to be out there cheering for our football team. But during this time, my skin color always felt like something holding me back. I wasn't sure whether it was something in my own mind or something I sensed from others. I kept telling myself it didn't matter, but I knew it did.

9

THE SCHOOL BOARD

BY THE TIME I WAS a cheerleader, Momma was practically a legend in New Iberia and even outside of New Iberia. Four of her children were listed as plaintiffs in one of the country's most important lawsuits — *Brown v. Board of Education*. In 1954, the US Supreme Court issued a decision in that case, finding that racial segregation in schools was unconstitutional. Even after the court's decision, New Iberia schools stayed segregated for 15 years. Until 1969, New Iberia's Black schools didn't get the facilities or attention of the white schools. We didn't have special music programs or a nice playing field. The teachers at the Black schools were paid less than the teachers at white schools. Unlike New Iberia's white children, Black students didn't have buses to take them to school.

Momma fought for New Iberia's schools to treat white and Black children equally. For years after the court's decision, she attended school board meetings, hoping to hold the district accountable for how West End children were hurt by their policies, which were now violations of federal law.

The white leaders of New Iberia didn't want to integrate the schools, so school board meetings became especially rancorous. Some board members, all white men, wanted to make sure federal law didn't upset the order of things in New Iberia, and they came up with some inventive ways of keeping the upper hand.

One of those ways was to create pretexts for firing the Black teachers who had taught in the Black schools, so the district could refill the positions with white teachers. Early in the process of desegregation, Joe Dugas, a school board member from Laurierville, presented a resolution to the board that would require the district to retain and hire only those teachers who had certification from a four-year college program. Of course, almost none of the Black teachers had that kind of certification since, during Jim Crow, four-year colleges in Louisiana didn't accept Black applicants. Black teachers in New Iberia had learned their skills in community colleges, from other teachers, and by the seat of their pants.

Momma got wind of this resolution before it was even listed on a board meeting agenda. She always had her sources, usually white residents who supported her causes but couldn't be public about it. When the matter was put before the board, my momma was there at the meeting with a fire in her belly. I was 12 and, although she didn't talk to me about it afterward, I learned plenty from friends at school and a newspaper article.

The meeting room was packed for the discussion of Dugas' proposal. Although the proposal was designed to hurt Black teachers, few residents spoke in opposition. Black residents feared retaliation, having known so much of it during Jim Crow. White residents feared retaliation as well, though of a different kind. White people who spoke out for us could lose job opportunities and friends.

But my momma spoke her plain truth. She stood up there at the podium and threatened legal action and the involvement of the federal government if the board passed the resolution. At the end of her presentation, she went way out on a limb.

"Mr. Dugas, are you a Christian man? Because if I was sitting where you are sitting," she said, "I would have to have a heart of stone to support a proposal that is so obviously designed to hurt people who have faithfully served this community and its children."

Mr. Dugas replied. "Nigger Bitch, you will never sit where I am sitting."

The room was silent. No one answered. The next day at school, I heard some of the kids talking about it. It was a big thing in town, but I wasn't sure at the time whether the scandal was over what Momma said or what Mr. Dugas said.

Momma's advocacy for school desegregation in New Iberia paid off. In 1977, the federal government ordered a desegregation plan that included a new school board seat assigned to a member of the Black community. The community wouldn't be able to exclude Blacks from public office. My momma ran for a seat on the school board and won. Momma was the first Black resident to sit on the school board and the first woman. When Momma was first elected to the board, the president of the board gave her a large binder with a policy manual. All board members had them. In her first school board meeting, Momma threw that policy manual in the garbage right there in public during one of the school board meetings. There were times during subsequent meetings that she reminded them she'd done that. She wasn't going to follow that manual, and during discussions in board meetings, she would refer to "Your policy. "She stayed in that job and drove the rest of them a little crazy for more than 20 years.

Not all of the white educators were racist. One summer, my brother Marcus fell in the tub into scalding water and was badly burned. Because of his treatment and injuries, Marcus couldn't go to school when it started up again in fall. Momma asked the school to help with tutoring so Marcus wouldn't fall behind, but the school turned her down. Momma asked for class materials to be sent home so Marcus could study on his own. The school administrator didn't allow that either. But a teacher named Mr. Sikes offered to tutor Marcus. After school, he would drive to the hospital in Lafayette, 20 miles away, with the materials Marcus needed, and tutor him so he wouldn't fall behind.

Thanks to Mr. Sikes, Marcus kept up with his school work for the six months he was recovering and passed the sixth grade at the end of the school year. My family kept in touch with Mr. Sikes until he died. In fact, his daughter tutored my son Ray-Ray many years later when he needed help in math.

The federal government didn't release Iberia Parish School District from oversight for many years because the board continued to propose and adopt discriminatory policies disguised as other things. They changed the school names if the names were of Black people. JB Livingston School became Park Street Elementary. The white board members would say it was because they had a new policy to remove names from schools. That wasn't true. Henderson High School, named after a Black man, became Anderson Middle School, named after a white man. They kept Hopkins School even though Mr. Hopkins enslaved Blacks. They didn't change the names of Pesson Elementary or Johnson Elementary, also named after white families.

Momma kept fighting. She recruited Black educators and consulted them about how to apply for a job. Some white members of the community would call my mom "racist" for trying to get equal treatment for the Black children in the schools. But she fought any kind of injustice. One day when I walked into our house after school, it was full of women, Black and white. They were school district cafeteria workers with stories of how poorly they were treated in the schools. My momma fought for them. She didn't care what color those women were. She knew that if you can oppress one group of people, no matter what color, you can oppress another one. She wanted the district's cafeteria workers to be treated fairly. At the time, the school board was planning to hire a white woman who had connections in the community but no qualifications to supervise the district's cafeteria operations. Because my momma made a fuss about this appointment, they didn't hire that woman and instead promoted one of the existing employees to the position.

The white school officials seemed afraid of my mom because the people in the West End would listen when she spoke and they believed her. My mom would knock you down but then she'd help you back up and, if she needed to, she'd knock you back down. If you were lying or cruel, she didn't believe in letting you catch your breath.

And when it came to Mr. Dugas, she got the last word. On the day she was sworn in as board member, she made a point to leave the building by way of a long hallway where formal photographs of deceased board members hung on the wall. She stopped at Mr. Dugas' photograph and glared at it.

"Mr. Dugas," she said, "I am here now. I am sitting where you were sitting."

10

LEAVING AND COMING HOME

I THINK EVERYONE EXPECTED ME to go to college after high school, but I wanted to serve my country. After graduating in 1978, I signed up for a tour of duty in the United States Army. I went to basic training in Jackson, South Carolina, and then attended Advanced Individual Training in Fort Lee, Virginia. I became a materials supply specialist, working on inventories of military supplies and equipment.

I was so happy to be in the military and serve my country. My good feelings didn't last long. During the first year of my tour of duty, I was assaulted by an Army officer who cornered me in an empty storeroom. It would be too painful for me to describe any more than that. I reported the assault immediately to my commanding officer, who told me that reporting the incident to higher authorities would compromise the group mission. I'd be responsible for undermining confidence in the leadership. This was his way of telling me my military career would end if my complaint went any further.

Instead of fighting like my momma would, I tried to ignore the trauma and pain. After that, I had a fear of being confined to spaces and felt a lot of anxiety, even in the best of times. Sometimes I felt like a prisoner in my own body and I had a hard time being vulnerable. I tried to hide it from the people around me, but I always felt alone.

My first assignment after Virginia was at a US military base in Wiesbaden, Germany, where I attended training in criminal justice. I didn't know it at the time, but that training would be useful to me years later. I loved my work in Germany. The land and the towns around the base were beautiful and I felt I was contributing to something important. I made friends and met Ray, the man I would marry.

I met Ray when he was a truck driver in the infantry. Ray was, yes, tall, dark and handsome. More important to me, he was kind and caring, protective of me like a big brother. I needed that after the assault. I was afraid to stay in the military, but it was what I always wanted to do. So I needed to trust the men in my life in Germany.

Ray and I got to know each other over a couple of years. The first time we went for a walk, I sat down on a swing in the park. Ray pushed me so I was flying through the air, feeling like a child and free. One time,

I showed up for a date in white painter's pants which were popular at the time, but I knew even then looked a little silly. Ray whistled at me and we laughed. We'd go to the movies or bowling on the base. Sometimes, he would leave the Wiesbaden military base for a couple of months on battlefield training assignments, and I found myself missing his company.

In early 1980, Ray proposed to me and we took the train to Copenhagen to get married. The weather was cold. We rode the train for two days through beautiful fields of blooming tulips. The day of our wedding, I went to McDonald's and got a Big Mac. Then I threw it up. I was so nervous we almost didn't get married. I loved Ray and we were best friends, but I wasn't sure I wanted to be married.

It wasn't long before we had our first child, Ray-Ray, who was born while we were still in Germany. I wanted to stay in the service as a career professional. I believed in what I was doing, but I knew it would be hard on the family if both Ray and I were on active duty, especially if I was deployed. At that time, there wasn't much help for enlisted women with kids. I knew I had to set aside what I wanted to do with my life and I left active duty to be a good momma. I joined the Army Reserves and Ray stayed in the army for seven more years. After Wiesbaden, we were transferred to Fort Polk, Louisiana, where our second son, Wendell, was born. Then a year later, we were back in Germany. Every time Ray was transferred, I got pregnant. I told Ray I wasn't going to drink the water at the next place.

Ray was still in Germany when I came back to the States. I stayed in Ray's hometown in North Carolina for a while with his family until he returned. Our marriage had been under stress from the instability of his many deployments, as many marriages become in the military.

After Ray returned the States, I got a job with Habitat for Humanity in Americus, Georgia. We were near Plains, Jimmy Carter's home town, right after he lost the election. I saw his beautiful house. I also saw real poverty. Plains was cut in half by railroad tracks just like New Iberia. On one side of the tracks was a low land called "The Bottoms." After the level of welfare in Germany, what I saw there shocked me. As a small child in New Iberia, I knew we were poor, but this was something else. The houses were unpainted and falling apart. They had outhouses out back instead of bathrooms inside. I could tell some of them didn't have electricity because there weren't any wires running from the poles to the houses.

One day, I was out walking with my friend Grace. We saw a very old woman on her porch in a rocking chair. She looked so tired and broken down, wearing a worn muumuu dress. We stopped to say hello, and she responded to Grace with "yes, yessum," as if she was a lesser person than my white friend. I had just come from the army where you raise your hand to serve the country. You don't know who you are fighting to protect your country. You are just protecting your country and the people who are in it. I saw more clearly all the discrimination in my country and how people identified each other. I didn't understand the depth of it until then. Georgia felt like a third world country. I saw what poverty looked like and smelled like. I nearly cried leaving that house because I had no idea people in America lived like that.

What I saw in Georgia made me want to make my own community a better place to live. I felt a new purpose. I wanted to do the kind of community work I saw my mom and dad and others doing when I was growing up. I knew if I could do it in Georgia, I could do it in the community that nurtured, protected and loved me as a child. It helped me understand who I am in my soul and it gets me up in the morning.

So I guess it was Plains, Georgia that got me back home to New Iberia. I had this new commitment to my West End community and I missed my family. While I was in Germany, my brother Boo drowned in Lake Charles. He was a strong swimmer but he'd been overtaken by a wake from a boat that swept him 200 feet from shore. Since he was such a good swimmer, his friends thought he was playing around when he yelled for help. I missed the funeral and I missed giving my family support in their grief. After that, I promised myself I wanted to be with my family in times of joy and grief.

When I did get home in 1985, I wasn't expecting to see how much things had changed in such a short time. This was during the Reagan years. If I hadn't been in Georgia, I wouldn't have understood what I was seeing, what the railroad track meant. I would have seen the poverty and the racial divide. We always had those, but we once had community. Now, I felt an unfamiliar sense of loneliness and fear that seemed everywhere in the West End.

The ways New Iberia had changed also changed the way people lived their daily lives. When I left for Germany, the West End had lots of mom-and-pop businesses, like a meat market, a pharmacy, shoe repair shops, dry cleaners, and bakeries. You could get what you needed by walking. We had community spaces where the older local residents played cards and shared stories. My daddy would bring home fish sandwiches from one of the cafes run by one of our neighbors. When I returned to New Iberia in 1985, most of it was gone. People from the West End had to go to the white part of town, to malls with big parking lots and Dollar Stores. So many of the houses were falling apart or were empty. No more mom-and-pop stores on every corner, and not much that made the community united.

There was nothing that was special. Only things that would hurt the community, like liquor stores and fast food. It seemed like a dumping ground. Abandoned industrial sites were polluting the ground and creating hazards for the children. Drugs were taking the place of the kinds of businesses that we wanted.

The older people in town talked about how this happened slowly but surely after the repeal of Jim Crow when local government agencies started imposing rules and regulations and taxes on mom-and-pop businesses in the West End. The parish Board of Health would target the cafes where the owners were just neighbors cooking for neighbors. They'd never had any problems. The local tax authorities went after people who were used to buying things and reselling them. They'd never been told about licensing or reporting requirements. The rules weren't even published. Many of the store owners couldn't even read. They didn't have lawyers and accountants. The city officials didn't help them, only harass them, so they went out of business.

At the same time, the white side of town was doing so well. Everything was still beautiful. Main Street was coming up. There were no liquor stores, no businesses that would hurt that part of the community. Most white families had cars, so they seemed to like the giant new stores on Admiral Doyle drive and south of downtown.

I brought my children back to a place that wasn't nurturing or safe as it had once been. When I was growing up, we didn't worry about crime. After I returned, I worried whenever my children wanted to ride their bikes. In its own way, it was once beautiful, but it wasn't that anymore. Some of the people representing the community knew what was going on but no one was doing anything about it.

Seeing what had happened to New Iberia, I felt a little responsible. So many in my generation had moved away for jobs and something better. I thought maybe we had some responsibility for the problems in our community. There were so few people left to take care of the community and our aging parents. People complained and blamed each other for the problems. There were plenty of people to blame, but I decided blaming wouldn't help. I wasn't sure what I could do, but I would do something, even if it was just a small contribution.

During this time, Ray and I went through a rough patch. He stayed behind in North Carolina where he had a good job, so I was with the children on my own for those first 4 years back in the West End. He would come to stay with us during the Christmas holidays to see the children. It was hard managing everyone and hard on the children. I knew part of the problem was that I was still in trauma from the sexual assault in the military. It followed me around like a cloud over my head. I got counseling and Ray moved to New Iberia. We made a commitment to working harder on our marriage, and we did.

All of this helped me understand that you can't know what people are going through. Most people have pain from something in their lives. People get dressed every morning and go out in the world, but underneath what's covering them, they're hurting. I was like that. I could smile, but underneath I felt like I didn't have value. I was assaulted and then demeaned when I needed protection. I learned to be quiet and I feared what could happen to me, believing no one would help me. For years, I kept it to myself, but Ray loved me and he saw me through it.

11

DADDY

I WAS NEVER MY MOMMA'S girl growing up. I wasn't a fighter like Momma because we had always been told as children that when we had a problem, and momma would handle it. I was mostly daddy's girl. My oldest sister used to laugh and call me Mother Theresa because the older I grew the more my servant heart began to shine, like my daddy's. Daddy raised us to be respectful and avoid conflict. I loved to read books and most time I behaved myself.

The people in town called my daddy "Mr. Mello." He was quiet and measured. My daddy would tell me stories about his childhood. The family was still living on the land at Little Bayou when Daddy was growing up. He was the baby of the family and the adults spoiled him. His momma, Bertha, wanted him to be educated. He was supposed to go to school every day but he would miss the school bus on purpose. He would hide under the bridge until the bus came and then head back to the fields. He wanted to be in the field with his big brother and the other boys, planting and chopping and burning sugarcane on the Carrier land. One time, he almost lost an eye when a tractor fell on him. After that, he was always a little cross-eyed but still handsome as ever. He only had a sixth-grade education but he was always trying to educate himself. When I was growing up, everyone assumed he'd gone to school for many years. He read and listened and paid attention to the world.

When I was little, Daddy worked at a radio service center and, later, became the first certified Black TV repairman in Louisiana. The den in our house was always full of broken TVs. He would repair them after he got off work. Most folks couldn't pay him, so they'd take their fixed TVs home and pay him a little at a time. Maybe someday they could pay him the whole thing. My daddy didn't care. He believed it was what he owed to the community and people who had more troubles than we did.

Daddy always dressed well, and he paid a lot of attention to how we kids were dressed. Sometimes people thought we had money, but we didn't. My daddy just had a lot of pride.

My daddy's real passion was to feed whoever was hungry. He taught himself to cook like a chef and opened the Carrier house to anyone who needed a meal. His rule was you made enough for everybody and if you didn't have enough, you shared what you had. Some of the kids in the neighborhood were so poor they weren't getting enough to eat. They knew they could come to our house at 5 o'clock. They knew what time the family ate. My daddy fed them. He cooked for people at funerals and weddings and fundraisers. Whatever was going on, my daddy was working at a booth barbequing chicken or frying fish. He would buy the food, cook, and never take anything for it. After I had my own family, my daddy would make food for us to pick up on the way home from work.

In 1995, Momma took all of us to the Bayou Classic football game in New Orleans like she did every Thanksgiving weekend. By then, Momma and Daddy were divorced, but they were best friends anyway, and Daddy always joined us for the game in New Orleans. That year, Daddy told Momma he didn't want to go. My daddy loved those games and being with the family. We should have known his staying home was a sign of trouble.

The next day I had a strange feeling about my daddy in the middle of the day. At the time, Ray and I were working at Martin Mills. We'd gone to work as we usually did, but I clocked out at 1 pm and went to check on my daddy. When I arrived at his house, the front door was unlocked and Daddy was in bed. Normally he would have been watching soap operas and cooking, but he said he didn't feel well enough to get up. I offered to take him to the doctor. "No," he said. "Ray is going to take me Wednesday for a checkup at the VA hospital." I felt a cold shiver go through me. I knew he couldn't wait until Wednesday and convinced him to go to the emergency room.

I walked to the Parks and Rec office, where my momma was working as a supervisor. I told Momma I needed her car to take Daddy to the hospital. I told her I thought he was dying. Momma was shocked at what I said, but I knew my daddy and, without directly saying so, he'd told me how sick he was.

By the time I got back to Daddy's, he was throwing up black dried blood. We drove three hours to the VA hospital. We couldn't afford the hospitals in town and the VA hospital didn't have ambulance services. By the time we arrived, Daddy was in terrible condition. The doctors took him to do some tests, and asked me whether he had a living will. I said no, he didn't. I knew what they were telling me.

At work the next morning, I got a call from the hospital. The doctor needed my permission to do exploratory surgery. We went back to the hospital to be close for Daddy's surgery that evening. Daddy's girlfriend and mom came. We sat in that waiting room for a long time until the doctor came in. He told us Daddy had advanced stomach cancer and they couldn't stop the bleeding. By this time, I felt at peace with it and I wanted my daddy to be at peace as well.

I was sitting next to Daddy when he woke from surgery. I told him, "Daddy, if you can hear me, squeeze my hand." He squeezed. I saw a tear fall off his cheek. "I know you love me, Daddy," I said. He didn't speak but he shed more tears.

That night, he told me how my great-grandfather had been the victim of a "terrible injustice" involving the family land and oil at Little Bayou. In 90 years, no one in the family had sought reparation. By then, I had figured this out, but no one had ever said it to me like that.

"I couldn't fix it. But you can fix it."

I didn't believe him but I said, "Of course, Daddy, I will make things right."

Ray and I had to be at work the next morning, so we drove back home. On the way, as we passed the sign for the Ville Platte exit on the highway. I felt something touch my left shoulder. I looked up at the sky. I could hear my little brother Boo say, "I got him."

The next afternoon, Ray and I went back to the hospital. When we walked through the swinging doors of his ward, we heard my sister screaming.

12

THE CITY SERVICES WE WANTED

During this time, I was working in my community, as I promised myself I would. I was up against a lot, more than I initially expected. We were 40% of the city's residents with the lowest incomes and the most civic problems, but almost invisible when it came to city services and our influence.[14]

One of my first projects was to fight the mayor's plan to replace an experienced supervisor named Lumpy Dominic at the West End park building. Everyone in the West End knew Lumpy and loved him. He had committed his career to the kids in the community. Mayor Cliff Aucoin announced he would replace Lumpy with a white woman named Kimberly Hebert who was a high school senior at the time. She was also the grandchild of our parish sheriff, Sid Hebert.

I was suspicious about how an 18-year-old had the qualifications to manage a recreation program, so I got a copy of Kimberly Hebert's resume. It seemed to show no experience relevant to the job, and the experience listed seemed exaggerated. And it was. She claimed to have been an "aquatic director," but I could only determine that she had been a lifeguard. She claimed to have run a daycare center, but I called the daycare center and they said they didn't know her. She also said she had run a beauty pageant. The only thing I could find out about this was that she'd been a contestant in the pageant. This appointment looked like a way of doing somebody a favor at the West End's expense and Lumpy's.

I rounded up a lot of people from the West End to support Lumpy at the Council meeting where Hebert's appointment was going up for a vote. The room was packed that night. Many of us got to the microphone and said how well Lumpy had served our community and its children. When it was my turn, I asked the mayor for an investigation of the experience Hebert had listed on her resume. The council later voted down her appointment. I don't recall whether they said anything about her resume. I assumed that was their way of saving face because they had to know she couldn't have done all those things by the time she was 18 years old.

Mayor Aucoin died shortly after that meeting. Some people said he took to his bed after the council meeting and never got up because that was the first time anyone had challenged him in public. He lost the vote on his proposal because of a Black woman.

My next project came soon after, because the City, without any notice to residents, closed one of its service hubs near the courthouse in the West End. The office had provided information about how residents could qualify for city, parish and state services. It was a place near our homes where residents could pay utility bills, get food stamps, apply for housing services, visit a health clinic, and other things. The City moved related city operations to an office on Bayard Road, three miles away along an open stretch of highway. Moving the office hurt the poorest and the oldest worst. Many residents didn't have a car and the West End didn't have any public transportation. People complained but the damage was done.

I wasn't going to let it go.

Ruth Fontenac became mayor in 2001 after Aucoin died. I asked her for a place where we could set up information about government services and applications in the West End. I explained that many West End residents couldn't get out to Bayard Road and suggested we use a small trailer on the corner of Shot Street and Anderson. Mayor Fontenac said she wanted me on her side, so she arranged to have the City fix up the trailer. She hired me to manage the program as resource director for the neighborhood. At first, I was part time and then later they made the job full time because there was so much need in the community. West End residents came to apply for food stamps, housing, and other government services. This made our community more self-sufficient and gave residents more opportunities to take advantage the services they were entitled to. It wasn't long before a new mayor came into office. The City shut down the program and I was laid off.

Getting involved with the City made me wonder whether much had changed during my lifetime. Jim Crow laws had been removed from the books, but the local government appeared to have simply moved on to new ways of hurting our neighborhood. It was just one thing after another, especially during the time Barack Obama was president.

First, the Parish bought some land about a mile north of the West End out on a big empty field, then announced plans to close the library in the West End and build a new one on that land. The library was nothing fancy, just a room in the community center with not that many books. But it was important. For years, West End children walked to that library after school to study, and it was full of kids almost every day. This was before the internet so the kids were relying on the library's encyclopedias and others books for their school work. The new library would require them to leave their neighborhood and cross the dangerous railroad tracks. The new library was located in a big field, where there wouldn't be eyes watching them.

Momma fought the closure of the library. As a member of the school board, she knew closing the library would hurt the kids. She went to City Council meetings and made sure the people in the West End joined her. She lost that battle and they built the new library. As we expected, most of the West End kids stopped using the library because parents worried about their safety. These days, the library isn't used very much, certainly not by West End students.

The West End used to have a program funded by a federal grant that helped low- income families make health and safety repairs to their houses. People needed these programs, especially the older residents who couldn't even afford to replace a window after a storm. In 2008, the City got in trouble with the federal government for the condition of its sewer system. So the City reallocated the federal grant money from low-income home repairs to rebuilding the sewer system. The grant was supposed to be allocated back to home repair services after two years, but it never was, even after our sewer rates doubled.

We were trying to make things work as we went along. It was hard enough just getting through the day sometimes without the City coming up with new ways to keep us from getting what the folks on the other side of town were getting.

The City also stopped the recreational programs it sponsored in the West End. It paved over the neighborhood swimming pool. After justifying closing the West End pool for lack of funds to repair the pump, we heard the City used the same pump on the pool in City Park, across the bayou in the white neighborhood.

The City eliminated funding for the children's summer camp, and all sports and wellness programs, although they would continue to be provided in City Park. West End children who for years could walk a few blocks to attend summer camp would have to travel several miles through empty fields where the children might come across poisonous snakes, and then cross at-grade railroad tracks, and go over the bayou to a part of town where they would probably not feel welcome.

Around the same time, the City ended the midnight basketball program in the West End community center. The program had kept a lot of the young men off the streets and out of trouble at night. No one explained to the West End community why the program was eliminated. Several residents asked the City to reopen the community center for this program, but were turned down.

We also lost the tennis courts, which fell apart because the City hadn't maintained them.

There wasn't much we could do about the swimming pool or the tennis courts or midnight basketball, but we set up a summer camp for the children. The City didn't help us. We had to raise funds for the poorest kids in town. We applied what we knew about the City's summer camp to our own program and found some volunteers. The camp provided the children breakfast and snacks, and helped them with academic skills, sports, and art projects. The parents appreciated what we were doing, especially because so many of them worked long hours and couldn't afford childcare.

The City had other ways of making us feel invisible. The Bayou Teche Museum on Main Street will tell you its mission is to "preserve the history and culture of New Iberia." Actually it only preserved part of our history and culture. The exhibits talked all kinds of things, like salt, Native Americans, sugarcane, and Spanish history. It didn't share the history or rich traditions of New Iberia's Black community except to display a photo of Bunk Johnson, a jazz musician who grew up in New Iberia.[15]

The City's website also hurt us. It described local "demographics" not with references to race, income and age, but by sharing information on housing for the aging. It didn't describe Black history in New Iberia except to explain that, after the elimination of slavery, "the plantation system was completely disrupted." And it referred to Jim Crow only as "the man who came to dinner and stayed." It's bad enough for a person to say this, but my own city endorsed it. The City changed its website in 2018, eliminating all references to local history and referring readers to the US Census Bureau's statistics page. It described the city as "progressive" and a place of "joie de vivre." Of course, for most of us, it was neither.

The West End lost a lot of government services over the years, while the City always seems to be working on improvements in other parts of town. Mayor DeCourt once said something about this to the *Times of Acadiana*: "Government cannot give anything it does not take from someone else."[16]

13

THE CHECK

Shortly after Daddy died in 1995, I started looking into property issues, not really knowing what I was looking for or what I would need. Momma thought I was on a wild goose chase. When I told my sister, Dawn, that I'd promised Daddy I'd investigate what happened to the Carrier land, she only said, "You gotta do what you gotta do." No one in my family was going to help me with this. It was going to be too complicated and too stressful. I was afraid of how it might affect my family and I knew it wouldn't be a fair fight.

I was dealing with a lot at the time. I was grieving my dad's death, raising four children, and I'd lost my job. I didn't get very far with the research for several years. I didn't want the stress I knew I would feel if I started investigating what happened. I did things a little at a time and I thought I should talk to Uncle Murphy because he wasn't well. I needed any clues he could give me before he passed. By then, he was living in St.

Catherine's retirement home in Loreauville outside New Iberia. St. Catherine's was a nice place, quiet and clean. Uncle Murphy's apartment was small but comfortable with a little kitchen and living room. He made tea and we talked on the sofa for a few hours. We talked about family for a while and then I asked him what he could tell me about the Carrier land. He didn't say much, nothing I didn't already know. Because he wasn't well, it would have been difficult for him to share a lot of details.

But the significance of my questions wasn't lost on him. As I was getting up to leave, Uncle Murphy said, "Robby, I knew one day you would make those folks give back what they took." When he said that, his face changed, like he'd been relieved of a burden, and then he said, "You be careful."

After Uncle Murphy died in 2003, I got one of my first pieces of evidence almost by accident when I contacted Glen Romero about some money he owed my family. Every year for many years, my daddy, his siblings, and his cousins would get a total of $200 from Mayo Romero or his son, Glen Romero, for farming sugarcane on the Carrier land. Uncle Murphy would cash the check and pay each of the ten Carrier family land owners their $20 share. After Uncle Murphy died, I called Romero to tell him I'd be taking the annual check on behalf of the family. I didn't tell him at the time that the family wouldn't be renewing the agreement with the Romeros for their use of the land, surely not for $200 a year. I didn't know the value of the land, but I knew it had been assessed forty years earlier for $100,000.

During our phone call, Romero said Brian Lasseigne, the manager of Romero's farming operation, would get me the check. Then I asked him whether he knew about a document that appeared to be an agreement between Mayo Romero and Uncle Murphy to transfer Carrier property to the Romeros. Uncle Murphy had given me that document. He told me his signature had been forged, and we could prove it by comparing it to Uncle Murphy's signature on his marriage certificate. I didn't say this to Romero. Romero said he knew about the document transferring Carrier land to his father, Mayo Romero, in 1970. I said I couldn't find any documents officially transferring title to the land. Romero said he had the documents and he'd bring them to me later in the week. He never delivered the documents and I was never able to find any in public files.

A few days later, as Romero suggested, I met Brian Lasseigne to get the check for the land lease. He said he'd meet me in the parking lot of the convenience store called Food and Fun, a few miles out of town. I drove to the meeting with my cousin Fay, knowing I shouldn't do anything alone. When we arrived at the parking lot, Lasseigne was there in a large grey pickup truck. The Romero farm was called Belle Place Farms, and its logo was on the truck's door. An SUV from the Iberia Parish sheriff's department pulled into the parking lot right after Lasseigne arrived. The sheriff's deputy stayed in the car. I wondered why Lasseigne needed a police escort at this meeting. I suspected this was a way of intimidating me, and I knew how things could go if anything happened.

Lasseigne stood next to the truck and held out his hand as I approached. I thanked him for taking the time to deliver the check and asked him whether he had authority to sign documents on behalf of Belle Place Farms. He said that, as manager, he did. The deputy was still sitting in his SUV watching us.

"Then," I asked, "would you mind signing this document that confirms the purpose of the payment? But before you do that, please be sure to read it so you're satisfied that it's correct."

The document referred to the $200 check as payment for Romeros' use of the Carrier land. It stated Romero's use of the land would end after the sugarcane harvest, and specified that the payment did not resolve any potential legal disputes between the Romeros and the Carriers. Lasseigne spent a minute staring at the document, shrugged his shoulders, and signed it.

Then I asked, "Would you confirm the purpose of the payment by making a note on the front of the check? You would just need to write 'for lease of Carrier land at

Little Bayou' on the line where it says 'memo.'" Lasseigne nodded and I watched him write the note on the check.

That was it. I could hardly believe what I'd accomplished in just a few minutes. Previous checks from the Romero family could have been for anything since the Carriers didn't have any written agreement with them. This check and the note Lasseigne wrote on it provided evidence that Romero knew the Carriers owned the land, and that the Romero family had been growing sugarcane there.

Fay and I drove from Food and Fun to the library downtown where I made copies of the check and the note Lasseigne had signed. We didn't talk about it but we celebrated with fried chicken and Cokes.

Shortly after I met with him, I heard he was arrested on charges of an assault that had allegedly occurred some years earlier. This might have been a coincidence, but, as time passed, there would be a lot of coincidences.

14

THE PULMONARY EMBOLISMS

AFTER UNCLE MURPHY DIED, I stopped my research on the Carrier land for several years. It was just too stressful with everything else going on, raising my children and helping out in the community. By this time, I also knew that I needed some time to let things settle, to let what I'd learned in pieces come together in my mind so I understood what to do next.

Then, something happened that got me going again. I broke my knee. Ray and I were working at the Fruit of the Loom plant in St. Martinville, a few miles from New Iberia. We arrived at work every day at 6 am in the dark. One of those days, as we were walking toward the plant through the parking lot, another employee's car arrived through the gate and hit me. I was thrown into the air and on to the hood of the car.

I went to the hospital in an ambulance. I remember the doctors trying to get me from the ambulance on to a gurney. They were frustrated that I couldn't help, but

I couldn't move my leg. At the hospital, they put me in a brace and sent me home. They told me I could return in a couple of days. When I went back to the hospital a couple of days later, an x-ray showed that my knee was fractured in three places. They kept me in the hospital for surgery.

I was still in the hospital recovering from the surgery on my knee when the doctors were trying to get me to walk so they could send me home. I was in so much pain, I couldn't move. The doctors were upset again, but a nurse told me not to let them intimidate me. That night, I was hooked up to several machines. After I went to sleep, one of the machines started ringing because I was flatlining, The doctors came in and gave me medication to revive me, but I almost died. I'd had a pulmonary embolism, a blood clot in my lungs. I had surgery again, this time to clear up the clots in my lungs. I was in the hospital for almost a month. During that time, my doctor asked me whether anyone in my family had a history of related health issues because pulmonary embolisms are often genetic. I didn't know and I didn't think much of it until later.

While I was still recovering, Fruit of the Loom shut down its St. Martinville plant. The employees were organizing a unionization campaign and the company wasn't going to have it. One day Ray went to work as usual, and the gate was closed. We both lost our jobs. So did thousands of people in many small towns near New Iberia. Fruit of the Loom shut down half a dozen plants in the area, and later reopened them in places like Vietnam.

Because I was jobless again, I had some time to get back to work on the research about the Carrier land. I needed birth and death certificates for several generations of my family. This would help prove the continued ownership of the land since the time the federal government gave it to Louis Carrier in 1867. Once I had the documents, I could file a petition with the court that, in Louisiana, is called "succession." Landowners can file such a petition where land wasn't bequeathed in an official will. Again, Black families didn't have access to the documentation system in the courts for many years, so they couldn't change the names on land deeds when an owner died. The succession petition would ask the court to officially acknowledge the ownership of the land by the descendants of Louis Carrier.

Anyway, I was sitting on the couch a few weeks later when Ray came into the room with a large envelope. It was one of those sultry Louisiana days and I was run down after so much time being immobilized by injury and illness. I'd been getting a lot of large envelopes, so I didn't think much of the one Ray was holding. I assumed it was another birth or death certificate. I opened it to make sure.

Inside the envelope was a single piece of paper, a death certificate for my granddaddy, Alphonse Carrier Jr. On the paper next to the box that said "Cause of Death," were the words "pulmonary embolism."

This shook me out of my complacency. The cause of my granddaddy's death was nothing more than a medical fact but it was one that changed the way I thought about my family. It didn't matter that the thing I inherited from him was something that could kill me. What mattered was that he had given me something that connected us. My granddaddy had been a virtual slave in the sugarcane fields during his childhood. He lived on the Carrier land for most of his life, believing that what belonged to him and his children was being stolen from him, and knowing he was powerless to do anything about it. Now I understood how I was so much a part of what had happened to my family and the Carrier land.

It would have been easy for me to keep putting off my daddy's request to investigate the truth of what happened to the Carrier land. But reading my grandfather's death certificate gave me a little more courage. Feeling that connection to my grandfather brought the past into the present and gave me a new sense of responsibility to my family. I say 'a little more courage.' During that time, I was afraid. Just investigating what happened to the Carrier land would be trouble and there would be consequences. The US military had prepared me to fight a war, but not that kind of war. Blacks didn't challenge the white elite in my corner of Louisiana. But then, I thought of how my daddy and my granddaddy cut cane for pennies on their own land. They didn't give up and I couldn't give up.

15

RESEARCH

The week after my doctor sawed the cast off my leg, I was ready to get back to work investigating the Carrier land. For months, I spent several hours a week in public libraries and the Iberia Parish Courthouse file room. I read diaries and letters written by family members. My cousin Fay and I would go. We were close and she encouraged me to keep doing what I was doing.

None of this was easy. I didn't know much about how to find public documents and I wasn't sure what I was looking for. I didn't know whether the documents I needed were in the parish courthouse or the parish administrative offices or somewhere else. To keep a low profile, I went to parish file offices at odd hours and only for short periods. I didn't make a point to be friendly with anyone. I didn't want to be noticed, and I didn't want to encourage offers of help. And I couldn't ask for help. If anyone figured out what I was up to, I could expect trouble. An unsympathetic clerk might alert someone who would destroy or hide the documents I needed. Maybe my family's house would lose its water service or the tires on my car would be slashed. These things happened in New Iberia to intimidate people who didn't go along. Fay used to say "It feels like somebody's watching us" and we'd laugh, but really, we were a little worried.

Another thing I had to consider was the cost. I'd just been laid off from my job with the City. I had been running a successful program to connect West End residents with resources they needed, like food stamps and Section 8 housing. The City abruptly eliminated the program shortly after I started skulking around the courthouse files. Without that income, my family was barely scraping by. Every time I found a document that might help me understand what had happened on the Carrier land, I had to pay the parish offices $.75 a page to copy it. Sometimes I'd have to collect pennies and nickels to pay for the copying we needed. I tried to think of it as an investment in the truth. One day, sitting at my dining room table, Fay and I looked at the stacks of papers we'd copied and laughed about how many other things we could have done with all that money.

I started with what little I knew and that led me to other documents. I knew that, in Louisiana, the oil company would have needed to file something with the courthouse in order to drill oil or lease the land. So I went to the courthouse file room and asked the clerk how to find official records associated with privately-owned land. She showed me the book where such documents were filed for the land at Little Bayou. I went through it until I found a 1934 document with Alphonse Carrier's name on it, leasing the land to the Texas Oil Company for the purpose of sugarcaning and other unnamed activities.

Another document, dated 1936, authorized the Texas Oil Company to extract and purchase the oil on the Carrier land. The royalties for the sale of the oil were to be distributed to Mayo Romero instead of the Carrier family. I remembered seeing the plaque at the land that day when I went there with my daddy. The plaque had Texas Oil Company's name on it and was dated 1936. The puzzle pieces were coming together.

Another document assigned the royalties to Romero for $10 and was signed "Murphy Carrier," my uncle. That meant Romero would get all the benefits of the oil on the Carrier land for $10. My Uncle Murphy wasn't well-educated, but he would not have agreed to that. The signature was suspicious because it ran diagonally from the signature line. So later that week, I compared it to Uncle Murphy's signatures on other official documents, like the deed to his house and his marriage certificate. The signatures were not the same. Uncle Murphy hadn't signed that document.

In the same book, I found a lease of the Carrier land to Texaco. It was signed by members of three New Iberia families: the Duhes, the Schwings and the Romeros. No one from the Carrier family had signed it, although I knew the document was leasing the Carrier land by the coordinates it included.

A document signed in 1957 named Mayo Romero as the agent for the Carrier family in transactions that permitted Olin Gas Transmission Company to extract oil from the Carrier land. That document wasn't signed by anyone in the Carrier family but, as the named agent, Romero would have received all the royalties.

I needed my great granddaddy's papers of manumission and was lucky to find them. They were in Baton Rouge at the courthouse. When I asked the woman in the office if I could get a copy of the papers, she told me to come back later. Instead of being in a place that would be easy to access, those kinds of documents were stored in the courthouse attic.

During this time, I got a little help from someone somewhere. I was waking up every night at 3am when a voice in my head would come to me about the kinds of documents I needed and where I'd find them. I didn't know whose voice it was or where it came from. It got stronger after I started sleeping on the couch so I wouldn't wake Ray. In the mornings, I would go to the courthouse and go straight to what I needed. That voice told me where to go in the courthouse files.

As time passed, I found more documents that gave away my family's property. One, signed by Mayo Romero, sold oil and gas leases on the Carrier family's property in 1971. Strangest of all, a document in courthouse records showed that Mayo Romero bought the Carrier family's land in 1970 from someone named Charley Jones. This document was part of the office courthouse files, even though Jones wasn't listed in any filed document as ever having owned the Carrier land.

I found a document signed in 1998 by Mayo Romero's son, Glen Romero, and a representative of the SONAT Exploration Company. It promised to pay Romero almost $60,000 for granting rights on the Carrier land to conduct a seismic study.

I was shocked when I found these documents because they were evidence to support what my daddy and Uncle Murphy had told me. I copied the documents and put them in my china cabinet at home.

Of all those documents I found in the parish court files, none had been notarized or showed any evidence of being reviewed or approved by any kind of government official. It seemed they had just been presented to the parish court offices and filed away. Somehow the court clerk didn't require evidence to show that the documents were lawful before treating them as if they were.

It also seemed that the records people needed to assert title to their land were tucked away in the courthouse attic or in Baton Rouge. The records that included lies were listed in the tax assessor's files and easy to find right there on the first floor of the courthouse. It seemed anyone could put them there as if they were official files. These kinds of things put me on notice about how many people and places had to be involved in the kinds of trouble I was looking into.

I couldn't trust anyone here, including the parish tax assessor. My family had always paid the taxes on the land, so I went to the tax assessor's office to make sure the records showed that they had. The Iberia Parish Tax Assessor at the time was Ricky Huval. His files showed the Carriers were "primary" owners of the Carrier land and also that they owned none of the land. The files showed that the Carriers were fully responsible for property taxes on the land, but that the tax bill was being sent to someone in Georgia. I later learned the person in Georgia was an heir of the LaBourgeois family from New Iberia. There wasn't any explanation for why the property ownership records had been changed without official legal documents or why my family was shown as responsible for the taxes but the tax bill was going to the Romero family. I convinced Huval to change the billing address so my family would get the bill. I had a feeling that wouldn't be the end of it and it wasn't.

After I had names of people in town who'd claimed rights to my family's property, I spent some time researching stories in the *Daily Iberian* about the families who were named in all those documents. Those families were related by marriage and were wealthy residents of New Iberia. They were lawyers and business people. They rode in Mardi Gras krewes and owned commercial buildings. Their daughters were celebrated as debutantes and their sons were acknowledged as accomplished athletes and students.

These families had built their comfortable lives and status at the expense of my family. I realized my family was trying to get by in a world that hadn't changed so much since the time of my enslaved ancestors. The laws had changed and so did the ways of denying us prosperity and justice.

16

GHOSTS

I HADN'T BEEN TO THE Carrier land since the day I went with my daddy in 1985. Since then I'd uncovered a lot of history that made the land feel strangely unfamiliar. I wanted to see the land with my new understanding and the new connection I had with my granddaddy. So, on a cold Saturday morning in January 2006, I drove to the Carrier land at Little Bayou.

The Old Jeanerette Road was empty except for an occasional truck. On the north side of the road, fields of sugarcane stubble went on for miles. The other side along the Bayou Teche was dotted with suburban-style houses, square except for carports and plain except for strings of Christmas lights.

I knew I needed to be careful. The Romero family lived on the Carrier land on the north side of Little Bayou, near the Carrier family's abandoned house and across the bayou from the oil derricks.

I found the dirt drive to the Carrier property, not expecting to recognize it even after all these years. There were not many drives out there and I knew the one I was looking for was just past an old roadhouse. The roadhouse was there, boarded up and standing in a nest of weeds. I turned left in the direction of Little Bayou. When I got to the gate I pulled the car over and turned off the engine. I sat there for a minute with a knot in my stomach.

There was not much to see on that side of the bayou, mostly just what little was left of the sugarcane. Little Bayou was smaller than I remembered, probably about 30 feet across, but still lined with palmetto and cypress trees draped in Spanish moss. I walked through the dry dirt along the bayou and found a one-lane wooden bridge that connected a second, smaller road to the land on the south side of the bayou. I walked across it slowly, feeling like a trespasser on my own family's land. On the other side of the bayou, I could see the stand of live oaks and underbrush that camouflaged the mess of metal that pulled my family's oil out of the ground. I walked past part of the foundation of my grandparents' house, large stones covered in moss and weeds. I could feel its ghosts, not the ghosts of people but the ghosts of fear and hate. I sat on a rock for a few minutes in a daze. I felt a part of this land. It once represented freedom for generations of my family. For a while, it sustained them and protected them.

I walked further until I saw the chain-link fence that was installed after my grandparents' house burned down in 1954. The fence was more than 50 years old by now. It was never there for safety or privacy. It was there to keep us off our own land. The people who put it there didn't need money or legal rights to take our land. Just a chain-link fence.

I walked around the fence until I saw more oil facilities, spread out over several acres of land, built like silos and small power plants. A pumpjack was operating, making that eerie rhythmic noise of metal on metal, muffled by the surrounding scrub. Some of the gas lines looked like they'd been capped off. I wasn't sure exactly what they were.

The ground inside the fence was a patchwork of low-lying weeds and black goo bleeding from the clay earth. The breeze carried the metallic smell of the crude oil dripping from the equipment. I could feel it creeping up my nose and down the back of my throat. My eyes watered and I vomited what was left in my stomach from breakfast. I got back in the car and went home.

After that, the land was part of me. I held its story.

17

THE FIRST LAWYER

When I felt confident that I had enough documents to file a lawsuit, I started looking for a lawyer. I knew it wasn't going to be easy. Not many lawyers in Louisiana were likely going to represent a Black family against Chevron and three powerful families. I also knew legal action would almost certainly create risks for me and my family. But I wanted the truth. I wanted those people to acknowledge what they had taken from my ancestors and what they would owe to my children. I wanted them to clean up their mess.

Watching the television one night, I saw a commercial for a law firm 20 miles northeast in Lafayette. Amos and Garrett advertised that they represented clients in personal injury cases. I met with one of them and explained my situation. He said he knew of someone who could help.

A few days later, I got a call from Floyd Johnson, an assistant district attorney in Lafayette parish who also had a private practice. Floyd wanted to look at the documents and think about it before he decided to take the case. He knew it would be complicated and controversial. A couple of weeks later, he told us he was interested, and we got the rest of the family to approve of engaging him. My cousin Fay and I met with Floyd one day after he'd had a chance to consider the documents we gave him. We went to his house in Lafayette. There, on the floor of his den, our documents were spread out like a completed puzzle, with each document telling a story. Fay and I looked at each in astonishment. We had given Floyd the story and he had known exactly how to tell it. We loved meeting with Floyd. He was kind and smart, and understood the sensitivity of what we were doing.

Floyd also knew the community and how to round up more evidence of what happened at Little Bayou. One day, he wanted me to meet him at the Oil Center in Lafayette. The Oil Center was a small business district that mostly served the oil and gas industry. Floyd said he wanted me to meet a retired oil man named Ruffin Lowry. Lowry was apparently very powerful in the local oil industry, a lawyer and landman. We met Lowry at a table in the back of a large dining room. He was probably in his mid-eighties, well-dressed and composed. Two bodyguards stood next to him and two were standing at the door. Before we arrived, Floyd had given Lowry the maps of the Carrier land and some of the documents I'd found, so he knew the situation by the time I met him.

We talked for a while. He asked me questions that by then were easy for me to answer. Lowry told us he knew what went on at Little Bayou on my family's land because, as a young man, he'd worked there. He said the oil companies would go on the land at night and take the oil down the bayou on barges. That way, they wouldn't have to account for it or pay royalties on it.

He looked at me square in the eye for a few seconds. "How long did it take?"

I knew he was asking how long it took me to find those documents.

"Not long because I'm not done yet." He seemed to know what I meant.

Lowry died in 2013. He wouldn't be able to help us in the lawsuit, but his consultation gave me more confidence in what we were doing.

At one of our weekly meetings, I told Floyd I had a dream. I was walking through a beautiful place with two groups of people. I was lagging behind. We walked into a place that looked like an old stadium with columns. I had to lift my feet because I was walking on graves. We were walking up a flight of stairs. Everything was bright. Half way, I asked someone in front of me where we were. Someone said, "Jerusalem." The higher I went, the brighter it got. At the top of the stairs, I looked out and saw women who were wailing. They were standing at the feet of a man with white hair. I asked who he was. Someone said, "Joseph."

After I told Floyd about this dream, he showed me a plaque on his desk. It had his full name on it. "Joseph Floyd Johnson." Floyd started crying. We all knew that dream told a piece of our story. It was a very emotional moment for all of us.

That same day, Floyd and one of his colleagues from the District Attorney's office took us out to the Carrier land. It was raining. As we approached the property, I could see that the gate to the property was open and the locks had been removed. Floyd didn't explain this, but he'd had somehow accomplished this with a phone call. It was the first time in more than 50 years that anyone without a key to that lock could access that part of our land. This changed my feelings about the land again, like I could protect it and know it. It would need protecting. As we walked through the gate and down the dirt road, I saw two oil rigs 100 yards in front of me spewing black oil into the sky, like black rain. I felt a chill go through me and thought of how this site must have terrified my parents and their parents.

In 2006, Floyd filed a petition to open succession. The petition showed that the Carriers had continuous title to the land since 1876. We needed the court to acknowledge that before pursuing any other kind of legal action relating to the land. The petition identified me as administrator, which meant I represented the 13 family members who now owned the land together.

The court approved our succession petition in 2008. I was so relieved, believing we'd overcome the first big hurdle. In fact, I was shocked that we'd been able to accomplish something so important for the family and our prospects in a lawsuit against Chevron. With the approval of the succession petition, the no one could take our land from us.

But that didn't mean they wouldn't try.

After the approval of the succession petition, I went back to the tax assessor's office in 2009 to make sure the records were consistent with the court's order on succession. Ricky Huval was still the parish tax assessor and his records still showed the Carrier family owned 75% of its land. They showed the Romeros owned the rest. After almost a year, despite his records, Huval ignored the court's order.

Huval wasn't in the day I went to his office. I asked the receptionist for copies of what was in the property file. She agreed to copy the file for me later that day. When I returned to the office, she gave me a small file of documents that included an "abstract." An abstract is an analysis of titles and transactions associated with real property, and includes any contract or other documents that might be attached to the land. The receptionist mentioned that the abstract had been provided to the office that day by a local lawyer named Lewis Pittman. Lewis Pittman was representing Glen Romero.

The abstract Pittman dropped off in Huval's office that day showed the Romero family owned 25% of the Carrier land. According to the documents listed in the abstract, someone named Valsin who didn't hold title to the land gave the land to someone named Charley Jones who gave the land to Blanche Welcome Foster who later said she inherited it from Angelle Carrier. Angelle Carrier was my family. She died as a young child so she could never have owned it. Blanche Welcome Foster gave a share of land she didn't own to Mayo Romero. What a mess – the documents and names didn't match up and the abstract didn't identify any evidence of a legal transfer of the property to anyone.

I took the abstract home and put it away. I didn't let anyone know I had it for several years, believing it could create problems but knowing it would be useful at the right time. It would show that powerful people in the parish were trying to claim ownership of the land a court order found belonged to my family.

While Floyd and Fay and I were working on the lawsuit we were planning to file, the State of Louisiana tried to prosecute Floyd for a domestic dispute that had been dismissed years before. The case against him was dismissed a second time. A short time later, the IRS conducted an audit of Floyd's tax filings and prosecuted him for tax evasion. Floyd was convicted and sent to prison for a year. He lost his license to practice law and we lost our attorney.

I kept in touch with Floyd. If he made mistakes, he probably paid a price others would not have paid. Or maybe he didn't make mistakes. I never talked to him about it.

I was discouraged again, which was probably the point. I dropped everything for a few years.

18

THE SECOND LAWYER

At about this time, things got more complicated. My cousin, Karen May, served me with papers that would remove me from the lawsuit as administrator, the person representing the family. Without telling me, Karen took a vote of the heirs to the land on her side of the family and filed a petition with the court to change the administration. I was surprised Karen would do this without talking to me in advance. We had grown up together. On Sundays after church, my family would drive to visit Karen's family in Terrebonne Parish. The children on both sides of the family would play together all afternoon until dinner. We weren't really close as adults but we'd kept in touch and cared for each other.

Karen's legal move worried me because she didn't know enough about the documents or the land to know how to manage the case, especially with a new lawyer. She wasn't familiar with the legal process. or the Carrier family history. Still, I didn't fight what she was doing. I'd put things off, and I knew how much work and stress it was going to be.

Karen contacted me shortly after serving me the papers. She said she'd hired a lawyer named Craig Stewart. Stewart practiced in Houma and advertised that he wasn't afraid to take on the big corporations. Other than that, he didn't have any experience in oil and gas law or property law. He was a personal injury lawyer who didn't even practice in the parish. Karen said he was a family friend.

For three years after that, Stewart didn't do anything even though Karen told me she had me removed as administrator because I hadn't filed a lawsuit quickly enough. I asked Karen many times when Stewart was going to file the lawsuit and she was never sure. I think she was worried about it, but she didn't know what to do. I certainly understood how complicated the case was and the evidence I'd found to support it, but I don't think Karen learned much about the documents or a legal strategy. It went on like this until 2012, six years after I filed the succession petition with the court. Glen Romero was still farming the Carrier land for free, without any lease or agreement. The oil and gas rigs were still drilling oil on my family's property and someone else was getting the royalties.

I had to do something.

19

THE INDEPENDENT

I WAS DESPERATE FOR SOMETHING to happen because I knew the delays could affect my family's claims. I couldn't involve myself in filing a lawsuit as long as Karen was the administrator. That was the law. So I did the only thing I could think of. I contacted a reporter working at *The Independent*, a small Louisiana newspaper. I told him everything I thought might interest him, and showed him some of the documents I had. He understood the situation and he cared.

I hoped making the story public would buy some insurance. No matter what happened, at least some of my family's story would be told.

In January 2013, *The Independent* ran a story on the paper's front page. It described what had happened to the Carrier land, with photos of some of the documents I'd found, and describing why they were significant. The article suggested the family planned to file a lawsuit and named Craig Stewart as the family's attorney. Ruffin

Lowry was also quoted as saying he'd worked at Little Bayou for many years and that it was "common knowledge" Texas Oil was taking oil off the land in the middle of the night so they wouldn't have to pay some of the land owners.[17]

The story motivated some change, but not the way I'd hoped. At the time, Ray was working as a driver for a small oil company. The Friday after the news article was published, Ray's supervisor asked him whether he knew the person in the article because we had the same last names. Ray tried to put him off but some of his co-workers told him his supervisor had been asking about him. Ray had been in that job for almost 15 years, always playing by the rules and getting good performance reviews. He was one of the only drivers who could read. Later, Ray admitted he knew me and suggested the facts would speak for themselves. A few days later, Ray was laid off. He would never be able to prove anything, but we knew how things worked in Iberia Parish. I told Ray it was okay. He'd find another job and it was time he had a break.

It seemed that the paper was punished too.. Since *The Independent* had apparently broken the code of silence in New Iberia, the local merchants in downtown stopped selling the newspaper – not just the edition with the article about the Carriers, but all the ones after that as well. The paper went out of business a few years later.

I wasn't surprised Karen accused me of undermining her management of the case. She was probably right, but her management didn't seem very effective.

It would be four more years before work on the case would start again. Stewart stopped answering Karen's phone calls and didn't show up for scheduled meetings. Finally, Karen and I met with Stewart in his office. At the meeting, Stewart told her he wouldn't represent the family because he was too busy. A Carrier cousin in California was calling him and stressing him out by pressuring him to do something. He said he didn't want to deal with that any more. I got the feeling he was having personal problems as well. He referred us to another lawyer named Keith Mayo. Stewart told us he was an oil and gas lawyer in Texas.

I didn't know why we were getting a lawyer from another state and one that might be cozy with the people in the oil and gas industry. But it wasn't in my power to do anything.

PHOTO GALLERY

 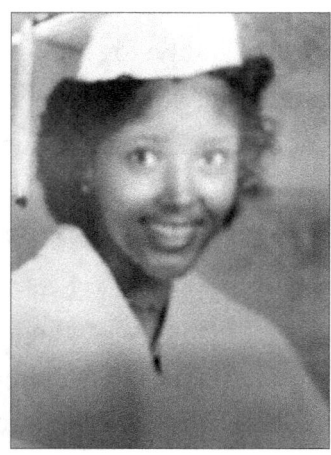

TOP LEFT: Clara Lee Degay Carrier, Robby's mother, during her years on the Board of the Iberia Parish School District.

TOP RIGHT: Robby Carrier Bethel at high school graduation

BOTTOM CENTER: Robby's high school cheerleading team

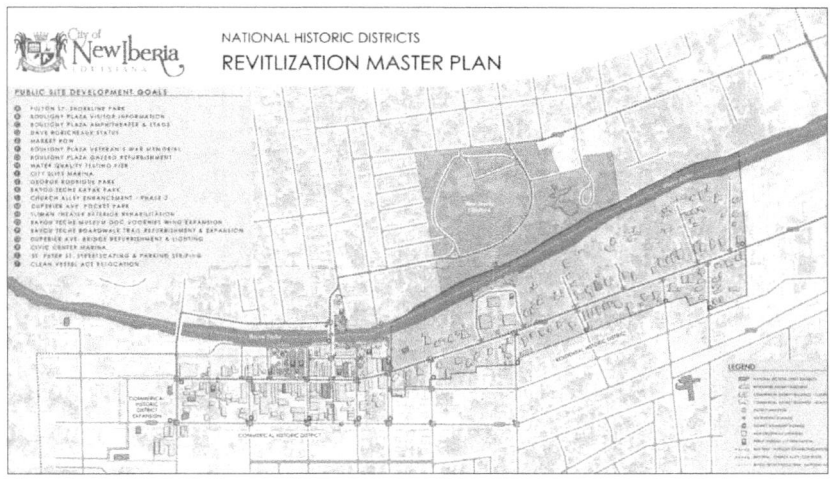

TOP: Melvin Carrier, Robby's father, at the barbeque

MIDDLE: Map of New Iberia from the City's Master Plan (Courtesy City of New Iberia)

BOTTOM: Operational pump jack on Carrier Land (May 2021)

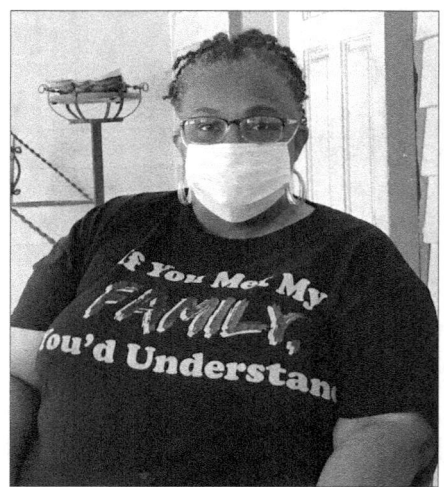
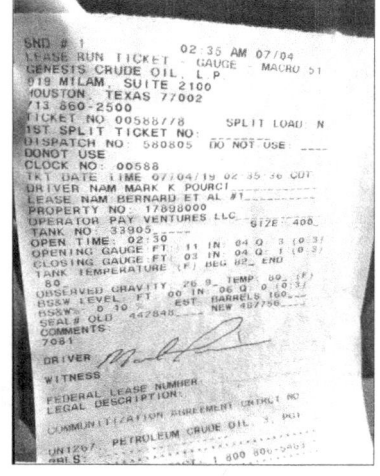

TOP: Mural of Bunk Johnson, New Iberia jazz musician, on the wall of Da Berry Fresh Market, Hopkins Street, New Iberia

MIDDLE LEFT: Robby during the pandemic, September 2020

MIDDLE RIGHT Ticket found in the mail box at the Carrier property recording petroleum pick up by truck driver at 2:35am, July 4, 2019, for Bernard 1 Well

BOTTOM: Map showing location of Bernard 1 well

TOP LEFT: Clara Lee DegayCarrier getting out the vote in New Iberia.

TOP RIGHT: Clara Lee Degay Carrier in her later years

MIDDLE: Mural in Iberia Parish courthouse hearing room

BOTTOM: Robby and husband Ray, 2023

20

FLOOD

Occasionally, the City would provide a service that people in the West End desperately needed and then eliminate it. We couldn't really count on the federal government either. The City and the federal government let us down in 2016, when New Iberia experienced one of its worst storms and the flooding that followed.

The West End was always prone to flooding during hurricane season, partly because of its proximity to the Armenco Canal near West End Park. When the canal would overflow, all that water would end up in the streets and houses of our community.

For years before the storm, West End residents begged the City to do something about the flooding. A lot of houses in the West End had been damaged over the years and we were already struggling just to get by.

Finally, the City installed a $4 million pumping system designed to prevent flooding from the Canal.[18] The pump was installed just before 23 inches of rain pelted Southwest Louisiana.

We thought that storm was some kind of sign, what you might call "biblical." It turned the West End into a lake, damaging or destroying hundreds of West End houses. People were climbing on their roofs and into attics to save themselves. Some lost everything and would have to replace walls and floors as well.

That $4 million pump the City installed was supposed to prevent the kind of flooding we had. After the flood waters subsided, West End residents asked the City why the pumps didn't prevent the flooding and we didn't get any good answers. Some believed city officials didn't turn the pumps on because they were worried that pumping the water out of the West End might increase the risk of flooding in the nicer white neighborhoods. The silence of city officials when we confronted them made us more suspicious that once again our city government treated one part of town differently from the other.

When the storm was over, parish and city officials didn't survey what had happened in the West End even though residents were begging for help. Because local officials didn't understand or didn't care how much flooding had occurred or the extent of the damage, it was a week before they issued a declaration of disaster. We needed that declaration because it triggered an appeal for help from the Federal Emergency Management

Administration (FEMA). But the appeal was so delayed that FEMA officials didn't arrive in New Iberia for almost two weeks after the flood. By then, West End residents had pulled together to make a lot of the damaged houses livable. Many had nowhere else to go, unable to afford hotels or airline tickets or repairs to the cars that had been flooded, so they had to take what help they could get and their needs were urgent. West End residents organized assistance to help those most in need, tearing out rotting and molding drywall, and removing debris and ruined furniture.

As a result of the work we did for our desperate neighbors, FEMA officials denied relief to many of the homeowners. Because some of the houses had already been repaired, FEMA accused some of the residents of trying to get help they didn't deserve, even though it was obvious many had lost almost everything they owned — clothes, kitchen appliances, televisions, rugs and furniture. Getting help from FEMA also required proof of ownership of the houses. Many didn't have this proof. In the West End, many people lived in houses that had been in the family for generations, and the residents had never gotten deeds listing them as owners. Those are called "generational houses," and people who lived in them didn't get any help. FEMA did help some of those whose houses hadn't been repaired by the time FEMA arrived in New Iberia, but those residents only got a few hundred dollars much later. It was too little and too late to help with recovery. We heard FEMA provided financial relief to many of the white families on the other side of the bayou. For many West End residents, the only option was to rely on our neighborhood association and a local non-profit agency to help with rebuilding. It would take us years to raise the money to repair all the West End houses damaged by the flood.[19]

21

THE THIRD LAWYER

The lawyer Craig Stewart referred us to, Keith Mayo, was fishy from the start. Although he represented himself to the family as an oil and gas attorney, it was hard to find out anything about his practice. I checked his website and his client list. He didn't have any expertise in oil and gas law or property law. His office was in a small town and he didn't seem to have any partners.

Mayo wasn't licensed to practice in Louisiana either. Louisiana law is very different from the law in the 49 other states. Other states have a system based on English law. Louisiana's laws are based on French law. Without training in Louisiana's legal principles, Mayo would be at a disadvantage against Chevron and three well-connected families. He wouldn't be permitted to practice law in Louisiana unless he could get the special permission of the parish court.

Mayo filed a petition with the court to be able to represent the Carriers in the Louisiana courts. They denied his request, probably because, as we would find out later, he was being investigated in the State of Texas. To retain his role as attorney of record, Mayo engaged a young attorney named Tregg Wilson from Baton Rouge. Wilson didn't appear to have any relevant experience either. His only associate was his father, who also didn't have any relevant experience.

All of this seemed suspicious. I worried that Karen still didn't seem to know very much about the case. She'd hired attorneys who didn't appear to have any relevant credentials. I didn't have any power to manage the case and I didn't want to start a family dispute, but I wasn't going to let it go.

Hoping to give Karen's side of the family a better understanding of our family history and the Carrier land, I worked with Karen to organize a family reunion. On the day we got together, we ate and enjoyed each other's company as we always did, but the main event was a trip out to the land. Most of the family on Karen's side had never seen it. I'd put my foot on it. I knew it from the time I was a young child, and that made a difference in how I felt about how it was being used and what we had to gain by pursuing our rights. Our visit to the land would be like a pilgrimage.

It was raining hard that day. The land was muddy and some of family members didn't want to get out of the van, so we drove through the gate on the south side of the land so everyone could see the pumpjack at work. Some of them cried when they saw it. Some of them were angry they hadn't known more about the land before then. My cousin Kevin picked up a fistful of greasy soil and stood there with it, getting soaked in the rain.

In 2017, New Iberia was named the City of the Year by Acadiana Profile Magazine.[20] This award seemed like a little bit of wishful thinking and obviously only applied to one part of the city. No one would give an award to the other part, but even downtown was showing signs of strain. A lot of small businesses had shut down after the development of corporate retail around the city's periphery, an area that was mainly two treeless boulevards of gas station and box stores built in the back of giant parking lots. There was nowhere to sit, walk, or ride a bike except in the midst of traffic. I thought maybe the award was for something in the City I didn't know about.

22

SISTER

Toward the end of 2017, I answered a knock on my door. A white older woman was standing at the bottom of the steps. She was short, wearing blue jeans and a black shirt. It's not often we get white visitors at the door, so I was a little surprised. She introduced herself as Kim Malcolm.

"I read the article about your family in the *Independent*," she said. "I'm interested in your story. Would you be willing to get together some time and talk about it?"

I wasn't sure what to think. She didn't say she was a reporter and she didn't have a Louisiana-way of speaking. I wondered how someone from another part of the country came upon an article in a local paper, and why she'd care about it. Still, I was curious.

We met and talked for several hours that week. I was cautious at first, but I remembered something my mentor once told me. "The Lord places like spirits in your path and you'll know them by the language they speak." Kim seemed to speak the language. She cared about what happened to my family, and she made me feel like I wasn't crazy for what I was doing. She was from California but traveling full time since retiring from her work in government. She wasn't a lawyer but she seemed to have a lawyer's way of thinking. Kim wanted to write a story about Louisiana because it was so different from other places in the United States.

One of the first times we talked, we were at one of the parish libraries. We were in a back room so we could talk without bothering anyone. I told Kim bits and pieces of what was going on with the lawsuit and the Carrier land. Every time we explained something, she would react: "You're kidding! I can't believe that! Why are you so calm? Don't you want to do something about it?" I sensed she had lived a very protected life because she didn't understand right off that when your life is full of injustice, you can't get worked up about every problem. You'd wear yourself out before lunch. Eventually, I think she understood that, although she never stopped using exclamation points at the end of her sentences.

Kim was in town for a couple of months that year and said she'd come back. And she did. We kept in touch after she left, but the following year, our friendship changed. One day she invited me to lunch and suggested we visit the African American Museum that had recently opened in St. Martinville, ten miles north of New Iberia.

Most of our get-togethers were conversations about difficult issues so I was looking forward to just having a nice outing. We ate lunch in a restaurant in St. Martinville. The weather was nice so we sat out on a patio overlooking the bayou, and ate salads and french fries. We talked about our children and our work like two people who hardly had a care in the world. After lunch, we drove across town to the museum.

We paid a few dollars for tickets and walked together to the main exhibit, past a life-sized mannequin wearing a brightly colored Mardi Gras costume. The museum was small, with painted panels dividing the room. People working in the fields had nice clothes and I don't remember seeing them called slaves. There were musicians and people celebrating holidays but no Ku Klux Klan. St. Martinville was once famous for its Ku Klux Klan. Nothing about lynchings or the poll tax. But I was so fed up I don't even remember much. I didn't want to stay, but I didn't want to say that to Kim, out of respect, in case she was enjoying herself. I hoped she wasn't enjoying herself.

I had to stifle my thinking as we walked around. The space was so small we could barely avoid each other. After a few minutes, I let my guard down and rolled my eyes just as Kim came around a corner. She was rolling her eyes too. I put my hand out and said, "Let's get out of here, Sister." Kim told me later she was holding back just as I was, out of respect, in case I was glad to have a positive portrayal of Black history. We laughed a lot about that day, both of us sneaking around trying to figure each other out.

After that, Kim told me some of her own story. For several years before I met her, she had felt powerfully connected to her own deceased grandfather when she was working with refugees in Greece. Her grandfather was a refugee who made it to California and then lost his whole family in the Armenian holocaust. Like my granddaddy, he couldn't talk about the pain he suffered or the oppression in the community of his homeland. He had to find dignity while feeling like a victim. I know Kim was also exploring her understanding of American racism after raising a Black adopted son, and as a descendant of people who enslaved Blacks in the 18th and 19th centuries.

I think Kim and I became close in spite of our very different lives because we shared some complicated feelings about our ancestors and our country and our children. For different reasons, I couldn't share a lot about my journey with my own family members, but Kim was always interested and helping me feel my strength.

I told her, "We've been here before. Together."

23

THE CITY SERVICES WE DIDN'T WANT

During that time when we were losing government services, the West End's economy suffered and that had consequences. Young men didn't have jobs and felt disrespected. There was a general feeling of frustration and injustice in the West End as well. Guns and drugs were easy to get. All of that contributed to increased crime, and that provided a justification for the kind of government services the West End didn't want — the kind of policing that made us feel like a bunch of criminals instead of a community needing security.

The sheriff's department especially has caused a lot of problems in the West End over the years.[21] One of New Iberia's most notorious sheriffs was Sid Hebert. He's remembered for, among other things, being convicted of polluting a local water source, getting arrested for drunk driving, and arresting an ice skating rink owner for playing rock and roll music.[22]

In 2006, Hebert's deputies caused a riot in the West End. Black residents had always been excluded from the town's biggest celebration, the Sugar Cane Festival that celebrated the harvest every September. The Sugar Cane Festival involves several days of partying, eating and music. It ends with a ball and the crowning of a court of sugarcane queens and princesses, all white in the festival's first 78 years.

Because West End residents never felt welcome at the Sugar Cane Festival, we had our own celebration, the Brown Sugar Festival, on the same days as the Sugar Cane Festival. It was an event for families and we never had problems with violence or bad behavior.[23]

In the morning of the 2006 Brown Sugar Parade, Ray turned on his police scanner. He heard the sheriff's deputies plotting to ambush the parade. They were sitting in front of the funeral home in their SUVs while people were setting up chairs on Hopkins Street for the parade and a DJ was setting up his equipment.

In the afternoon, the parade got going and everyone was peaceful and having fun. Then the sheriff's deputies began rolling their cars up and down Hopkins Street where the parade was held. Some of the deputies were walking through the crowd with their dogs, and they turned on sirens to drown out the music. They started harassing a young man and trying to arrest him. No one was sure why. When a couple of other men tried to calm things, the sheriffs deputies fired tear gas canisters into the crowd, including older people and children. Everyone was coughing and crying and running, trying to cope with the pain of the tear gas.

A few months later, West End residents sued the sheriff's department for abuse. Someone who didn't know the West End was put in charge of negotiating an out of court settlement. The settlement provided that the sheriff's department would set up a resource center in the middle of the West End. They set up the resource center, but almost no one would go in there. People didn't know what it was for and were afraid because it was associated with the sheriff and his deputies. That settlement did nothing to help the West End or stop aggressive policing against young Black men. The black SUVs continued to sit on street corners making everyone feel guilty of something. West End residents were afraid to call the sheriff's office to report crimes, knowing they themselves might become victims when the deputies showed up.

Hebert left office in 2008, but for ten years after that, the Parish sheriff, Louis Ackal, presided over what, for West End's young Black men, was a reign of terror. The brutality of his operation was so obvious that Ackal was indicted in federal court for allegedly overseeing the routine torture and persecution of Black men in New Iberia, and for using his office to settle personal scores, among other things. He escaped conviction in spite of the damning evidence against him, but seven of his deputies went to prison. [24]

During the time when Ackal was sheriff, my sons Ray-Ray and Wendell were young men. It was hard for me to let them drive the car by themselves because Ackal and his deputies were targeting Black boys. I slept on the sofa so I wouldn't fall into a deep sleep until my sons came home from a football game or a night out with friends. Until they walked in the door, I couldn't sleep. They were never troublemakers, but I needed to know where they were all the time. Sometimes we drove them to and from their friends' houses even if they were going only a few blocks away.

Even getting a haircut could be a risk. One time, Ray-Ray was waiting with his son, Latrelle, for the barbershop to open. The two of them were sitting out front in the family's white pickup truck. Out of the blue, the sheriff's deputies' SUVs surrounded them. The deputies ran to the truck with their guns drawn and pointed at Ray-Ray and Latrelle. They were aggressive and asked a lot of questions. They terrorized Ray-Ray and Latrelle before they realized they were looking for someone else. Then they left without any apology or explanation.

Ray-Ray and Latrelle were traumatized by that, knowing anything they did or said could have left them dead, because they knew what happened to Victor White. I knew about Victor. He wasn't a troublemaker and didn't have a criminal record. One night, the sheriff's deputies arrested Victor, allegedly for possession of drugs. The record is unclear and full of inconsistencies, partly because the cameras that would have shown what happened weren't working that night. After the deputies arrested Victor, they put him in the backseat of one of their SUVs. His hands were handcuffed behind him. That night, Victor died from a gunshot wound. The deputies later claimed he shot himself in the back while he was sitting in the police car. But the coroner found that Victor was shot in the chest. The police couldn't produce the gun they said Victor used to shoot himself and couldn't explain how Victor got hold of a gun. The case was investigated, and the findings were "inconclusive." Victor's death left deep scars in the West End. Eventually, Victor's family was awarded $133,000 in a settlement with the sheriff's department. The family's lawyer got $192,000.[25]

There were many other payouts to settle lawsuits against Sheriff Ackal's office. Between 2015 and 2019, the sheriff's department spent more than $6 million to settle lawsuits, plus the cost of its private attorneys. That's a lot of money in a parish of 70,000 residents, many of them poor.[26] And yet Ackal was elected every time he ran for office.[27]

Ackal left office in 2018, but the New Iberia police mostly picked up where Ackal left off. Now I worry about my grandsons. Not long ago, Ray-Ray's son, Terrelle, was at an annual festival on the other side of town, near the Sugar Cane Festival building. Terrelle walked there with his friends, but left early on his own so he could get home in time for a family dinner to celebrate his grandpa's birthday. Terrelle was limping through downtown because he was wearing a pair of new shoes that gave him a blister. A sheriff's deputy in an SUV pulled up beside him. Instead of asking him whether he was okay, the deputy asked him whether he'd been drinking. After Terrelle explained why he was limping, the deputy let him go. He told Terrelle he'd be "watching him."

Almost all West End residents had stories like these. In 2017, about 100 of us attended a public meeting with the mayor and members of the city council. We complained about how law enforcement treated us with hostility, even when we were reporting crimes in progress. City officials didn't say they'd work with law enforcement to fix the problem or that the police should be there to protect us. They suggested we report crime to an anonymous phone number they'd set up, operated by a private organization. This was an admission by our own public officials that law enforcement couldn't be trusted to protect our community. The residents of other New Iberia neighborhoods could call the sheriff's office directly. They didn't have to call a private company because they could assume they'd be safe when the deputies arrived.

These things created a sickness in our community, making people feel nervous and disrespected. Our young men often feel suspected of something. They know they can never defend themselves from accusations or violence. They are powerless. My family was lucky that our sons and grandsons survived the years of their youth, but they still live with the fear and youth was stolen from many others.

In a public meeting in 2020 about City planning, Mayor DeCourt offhandedly mentioned that some white residents of New Iberia were perfectly fine with young Black men in the West End killing each other. He didn't say what he thought about that.

It was in this world I was fighting some of my city's most powerful people. But I knew them and they knew I knew them.

24

ENVISION DA BERRY

WHEN I WAS GROWING UP, the preachers in town were advocates for civil rights. They were leaders in the West End, speaking out and defending the rights of the local residents. The pastors knew everyone and came to the houses to talk to children who were getting in trouble. They made sure the families in the community were safe and had food. We weren't rich, but everything the community needed was in the community and the churches were at the center of that, like gatekeepers.

By the time I got back to New Iberia from Germany and Plains, all that had changed. Some of the pastors seemed to be looking out for themselves ahead of the community. Over the years, some were given jobs in government or small contracts. They stopped speaking out and working for change. A lot of us think the jobs and contracts made them beholden to white bosses. People still went to church, but the churches stopped being the center of our community and we didn't have the kind of leadership the pastors had provided in earlier years.

This seemed to be a strategy in New Iberia's city government.

Around 2011, the neighborhood felt a little hope for good change in New Iberia when Phanat Xanamane moved back to New Iberia. Phanat was born in a Thai refugee camp, the son of Laotian parents who escaped the Vietnam War on a small boat. Phanat and his family settled in the West End. While Phanat was growing up, the family farmed a small plot of land, and eventually had an Asian food market on Hopkins Street.

I'm guessing Phanat was the kind of child who knew he would go to college, and he did, graduating with a degree in architecture from Columbia University in New York City. After that, he worked for the City of New York as an urban designer for five years. Phanat returned to New Iberia because he wanted to support the place where he grew up. He committed himself to ten years of community service.

Phanat was handsome, smart, and well-spoken. He was easy to like. I think he wanted to help create trust in New Iberia between white and Black, rich and poor. As a gay Asian man, Phanat understood what it was like to be an outsider. Shortly after he returned to town, he created a nonprofit organization called Envision Da Berry. Its mission was to "build creative businesses, establish cultural resources, and breathe fresh life back into our community."[28]

Phanat kept his promise to live in the West End for ten years, and during that time, he became a bit of a celebrity. He helped organize the Brown Sugar festival and marketed the annual Lao New Year's Festival. He was appointed to local committees and boards, and became a quiet resource for advice and ideas.

During his ten years, Phanat and Envision Da Berry created two enterprises, the center of which was Phanat's home on Hopkins Street. Phanat's house stood out on a street of run-down storefronts, abandoned buildings, and empty lots. The house had charm, brick with gables and nice windows. It had an Airbnb apartment, and a design studio. It was surrounded by shade trees and a large landscaped garden.

Behind the house, Phanat built an urban farm using some very modern techniques. He grew vegetables in vertically-layered buckets attached to plastic poles, and rows of kale and broccoli along the fence line. Inside a large warehouse behind the garden, he grew several varieties of mushrooms.

A few blocks down Hopkins Street, Phanat created Da Berry Fresh Market with a young man named Carl Cooper. Da Berry Fresh Market was a rare thing in New Iberia. In what had been a wooden garage, Carl painted the Fresh Market bright green with brighter trim colors.

One of the outside walls was painted with a mural of a rainbow and New Iberia's famous jazz musician, Bunk Johnson. The market sold fresh produce, hand-made jams and condiments, and pre-cooked grains in small plastic bags. Carl wanted people to have access to books, so he had free used books on a couple of shelves near the back of the store. Carl sold brightly-colored dashikis that were hanging from the ceiling, and beaded leather bracelets and essential oils. He grew vegetables in a small plot behind the store. Carl wasn't shy about talking to customers about his Rastafarian philosophy. I don't think a lot of folks in New Iberia shared his thinking on this, but everyone liked Carl. Da Berry Fresh Market was a bright spot on Hopkins Street.

I didn't really know much about these Envision Da Berry projects, but over time I knew enough to have some questions.

Early on, Phanat worked with the City to raise funds that were supposed to support West End projects. The City had created a special "historic" and "cultural" district in the West End. The neighborhood's economic decline and rich history was a made it a good candidate for state and federal grants, and it seems Phanat and the City got a lot of money for West End cultural district projects.

I heard some grumbles about this from a few of my neighbors and tracked down some City documents reporting on the use of grant funding. I found one City report from 2013 that stated the City received a $1 million grant from Blue Cross Blue Shield for West End projects. The City reported the funds would support a farmer's seafood market, community gardens, and "educational workshops on healthier cooking and the preparation of foods." It also reported that our neighborhood association, was part of the advisory committee for such projects. I'd always been on the board and we were never consulted about these funds or their use in the West End. More than that, it's not clear that any of the listed projects was ever funded. We never had a seafood farmer's market on our side of town and no one I know recalls cooking workshops in the West End.

I only know of two garden projects in the West End. Carl had gardens behind Da Berry Fresh market, but he once told me he didn't get any grant money for the market or the garden. Phanat's gardens on Hopkins Street weren't community gardens because they were never open to the community. They were located behind fences, and didn't offer West End residents access unless they were volunteers working for Envision DaBerry. The produce from the Hopkins Street gardens was too expensive for most West End residents, and I'd heard that most of it was sold to high end restaurants in Lafayette.

The only community garden I've ever known about - one that gave local residents a place to grow vegetables — wasn't in the West End but across town near a housing project. It was abandoned after its first season. A friend of mine who worked in the garden for a while said, "It only produced a few cucumbers."

It seems there was also grant money for an arts center in New Iberia that was part of a partnership between Envision Da Barry and the City. The City's 2013 annual report on the West End Historic District's grant-supported activities described a proposed cultural venue — not in the West End — that required extensive renovation, suggesting grant funds would be used for that purpose. The building, located downtown at 301 W. St. Peter Street, belonged to Freddie DeCourt. At the time, DeCourt was on New Iberia's city council and later became mayor. One way or another, the building got the renovations and became NILA Gallery in 2013. The Facebook page for NILA gallery showed it was an Envision Da Berry project for a while. Then, according to the Facebook page, sometime around 2016, the gallery closed and re-opened as a for-profit private events center called Bayou Teche Trading Company, owned and managed by DeCourt. In 2022, The Teche Growers Association bought the building and turned it into The Harvest Room, an events venue.[29]

That seems an appearance problem if nothing else, because I don't think grant money was supposed to be used downtown to benefit private businesses. But I don't know the whole story.

I had a hard time tracking down information about how other government funds were used that were supposed to go to West End revitalization projects. The City's budget doesn't usually show where money is spent by neighborhood. The City seems to have gotten some grants from the Louisiana Lieutenant Governor's Department of Culture, Recreation and Tourism. I did find some of the City's annual reports to that department regarding the progress of revitalizing the West End Cultural District. One lists West End projects that were actually organized and paid for by our neighborhood association, with no support from the City, including a mural on Hopkins Street. Other projects listed by the City in its 2014 report didn't benefit West End residents or take place in the West End. It listed an event downtown that provided pastries and coffee at the NILA gallery, a Christmas parade downtown celebrating a white artist, and a music event that took place in Breaux Bridge, 23 miles north. As far as I know, none of these events provided any benefit to the West End Cultural District.

At some point, Phanat and the City didn't seem to be working together so much. I was surprised when Phanat told me Mayor DeCourt didn't consult with him about what the West End needed before publishing New

Iberia's Master Plan in 2020. By then, Phanat was posting on Facebook about spending time on his mother's farm in Northern Louisiana.

Phanat ran for State Senate in 2023. He lost, but I wish he'd won. He cares and he's smart and he probably knows a lot more about government than most people in town. And I don't know what happened with Phanat's projects, but it seemed like something happened along the way that reminded me of those church pastors.

I'm not saying I know the truth of all of this but, from what I saw and read, I couldn't help but see a pattern of what looked like good people getting involved with people who didn't have the best of intentions. I would see plenty more of this.

25

THE LAWSUIT

I WAS TRYING TO KEEP up with all the City's efforts to disenfranchise the West End, and working with the neighborhood association while my mind was pacing the floor over the lawsuit. It was going nowhere. Karen's new attorneys, Wilson and Mayo, had the information they needed from the Carriers but didn't file anything for almost 18 months. There were unexplained delays. Karen sent emails periodically asking the lawyers to file the suit and she would get another homework assignment. Once, Wilson had asked for the birthdate of a long-dead ancestor. I couldn't think of why he needed that information and it wasn't used anywhere later. I wondered whether the attorneys were delaying the filing on purpose or building a case for someone else.

During our last phone call between the family and the attorneys, Mayo said he had everything he needed to file a lawsuit except one very important document. He needed a pooling agreement to show the Carriers were entitled to royalties. "I have that," I said. "It's dated 1916." I think he was surprised because he took a long pause before he asked to see it. I had a photo of it on my computer and sent it to him right as we were sitting there.[30]

At our last meeting with Mayo and Wilson before they filed our complaint, they explained what the complaint would say. What they read to us about the contents of the complaint sounded accurate and compelling, so we agreed they should file.

Finally, in December 2018, Mayo and Wilson filed the complaint in December against Chevron/Texaco, and the three families who had land adjacent to ours: the Duhes, the Schwings, and the Romeros. It was no cause for celebration for me. The complaint was not the document Mayo described to us at that last meeting. It was short and confusing. It didn't present a history of what the plaintiffs alleged. It didn't include any of the documents I'd dug up that showed evidence of fraud or ownership of the land. It didn't seek a procedural schedule or suggest what the plaintiffs would show with evidence. It didn't use words like "fraud," "conspiracy," "conversion" or "theft." I couldn't help thinking it was written in a way that would be almost impossible to interpret for anyone who wasn't a Louisianan attorney. Because I wasn't one, I wasn't sure whether even an attorney would understand it either.

Four of the five plaintiffs filed murky responses that included arguments against relief the complaint didn't seek; for example, saying we weren't entitled to royalties for drilling on a neighboring property. We didn't ask for royalties for drilling on a neighboring property. We had the pooling agreement that showed the Carriers were entitled to the same royalties as the defendants for drilling occurring on our own property.

The Duhe family never officially responded to the original complaint or any other pleading filed in the case. This failure to reply to the complaint arguably put the Duhe family in default – meaning it was effectively an admission of the allegations in the lawsuit. Our attorneys didn't raise this issue and the judge didn't either.

The lawsuit created complications for my family. I lost income. At the time the lawsuit was filed, I was working as a consultant for a local non-profit agency near New Iberia that helped with housing, disaster relief, and other social issues. The agency partnered with the neighborhood association a lot and gave our neighborhood association funding for projects. The people who ran the non-profit agency cared about social justice and what I was doing, but one of its board members was employed by one of the defendants in our lawsuit. I also understood the organization got funding either directly or indirectly from Chevron.

Shortly after we filed the lawsuit, a board member from the nonprofit agency told me, "Robby, the lawsuit doesn't look good for us." She didn't need to say more. I assumed she was asking me to resign. I didn't want to compromise their important work serving the community, so I resigned. I'd find other ways to support the community and my family.

The lawsuit also changed Ray. He insisted I always let him know where I was. If I went from the grocery store to meet with a friend, he wanted to know. He wanted me to call often. He was worried. By that time, Ray was retired so he didn't lose another job.

A year after we filed the lawsuit and following defendants' requests for continuances, the judge scheduled what, in other states might be called a "preliminary hearing." The purpose of such a hearing would normally be to plan the management of the case; for example, to discuss key issues in dispute, set a schedule and ground rules for the discovery process, and address matters that required briefings or mediation. Normally, the judge would have informed us in advance about the purpose or agenda of the hearing, with something in writing. He didn't do that, or, if he did, I couldn't find it in the case file at the courthouse.

So the Carriers didn't know the purpose of the hearing in advance and our lawyers didn't do much to prepare us for the hearing either. The family had a call with the lawyers where Mayo explained what he thought would happen in the hearing. He said he thought Karen and I would be called to testify about what we knew about the property.

The hearing was held on April 8, 2019 in the Iberia Parish Courthouse, which sits like a DMZ between the West End and downtown. At first glance, it looks like it was dropped into a parking lot by airlift. It's white. It's solid. It's shadeless and benchless and authoritative. It was built in 1939 by Franklin Roosevelt's Works Project Administration, part Art Deco, part Soviet. Some of its detail redeems it and then damns it. At the bottom of the three-story vertical windows on the façade are the words "Justice" and "Equality." As if to neutralize those words, inside the main courtroom, behind the judge's bench, was a dramatic floor to ceiling mural showing a tall, muscled white man standing over three smaller men who appear to be Asian and Black. They are gambling. One of them lies on the ground protecting his winnings. Sitting in that courtroom, there was no way to avoid the mural's demeaning message.[31]

The hearing was held in the mural room.

Just before the hearing, Wilson met with Karen and me in the courthouse parking lot. Wilson said the hearing was going to address whether Karen and Uncle Smithy had authority to bring the suit. He said all three of us might be called to the stand to testify. He didn't tell us much about what to expect or how to emphasize the facts that were most important to our case, but he did suggest I was an important witness because of my knowledge of the documents and the land.

Judge Sigur opened the hearing by asking the parties to identify themselves. No one attended representing the Duhe family, which the presiding judge didn't note. This seemed fishy, an acknowledgement that the District Attorney could decide whether or not he could be sued. Judge Sigur told us that the main topic of the hearing would be the one described in a February 21, 2019 letter submitted by Chevron. I'd never seen it and neither had Karen. The letter wasn't read into the record and later, when I looked for the letter in the proceeding file, there was no copy of it.

I was sitting there thinking we were completely unprepared for a hearing held according to Chevron's agenda that could determine my family's claim that it had been cheated for more than 100 years.

At the beginning of the hearing, Chevron's attorneys put a large posterboard on an easel. The posterboard showed a page from the succession petition I'd filed years before. I was never clear on what purpose was served by the posterboard or the reference to the succession petition. Maybe they just needed to bring something to the hearing to make it look like work. The two Chevron attorneys were very young. They didn't bring any files to the hearing. They didn't seem to know what they were doing. I think they came to that hearing knowing they didn't need to do much of anything.

The judge didn't say much during the remainder of the hearing and I never thought he had control of the hearing. He let Chevron's attorney run the show. He began by presenting an argument on the issue of "prescription," which in the laws of other states might be called a "statute of limitations" or "laches." All three legal theories set limits on how long a plaintiff can wait to file a lawsuit. The amount of time usually depends on what the allegation is, and there are exceptions to the time periods depending on the circumstances of the case. When Chevron's lawyer was arguing that we waited too long to file a lawsuit, he didn't mention that Chevron was still pulling oil out of the land.

In any event, prescription is a complicated area of law and, in our case, whether it applied depended on some complicated facts. Wilson had previously made this point. Then, during the hearing, Wilson raised the issue again, and asked for an opportunity for "discovery," which would permit the Carriers to track down evidence and present it to the court. According to the transcript, the judge didn't reply to this request. But I remembered Chevron objecting and the judge overruling the objection.

After Chevron's attorney argued the legal issue of prescription, Wilson called Karen to the stand. Karen testified she had never been on the land before she became administrator of the litigation in 2017. She said a previous attempt to enter the land was impossible because it was behind a locked gate where a guard was stationed. Wilson seemed to be making an effort, but he wasn't in command of things. Karen's testimony was incomplete and Wilson just let it go. I sat there feeling just sick to my stomach.

During the hearing, the Judge granted Wilson's motion to file in opposition to Chevron's claim that Karen didn't have standing to bring the case. I never really understood what that was all about. She was the administrator for the family and the court had approved her role in the lawsuit, so I wondered how someone could argue she might not have standing. The judge set May 23, 2019 as a briefing date on that issue.

The Carrier family lawyers never fully argued the issue of prescription — that is, whether we waited too long to bring our case to court — or ask for an opportunity to brief the issue, even though in the hearing Chevron was building a case for that. I didn't need to be a lawyer to see that. Up until the end of the April hearing, I believed Wilson was trying. He had asked for discovery. He tried to argue the legal points raised by Chevron. After the hearing, Wilson filed a very short brief on

April 29 demonstrating Karen's authority to represent the family. It included official court documents giving her that authority, which I thought had been there in the case file all along.

After that, Wilson seemed to give up. He never conducted any discovery or showed how it would help us prove our case. He didn't push to file a brief on the issue of prescription or how it related to Karen's testimony. He never filed anything else either, even though he would have opportunities after the hearing to advocate for us.

26

THE JUDGMENT

Momma had been diagnosed with early onset dementia sometime around 2012. It was hard to see her slowly lose her ability to analyze situations and communicate. Those things had defined her all my life. As time passed, her condition got worse. She'd repeat questions she'd just asked or forget something she'd been told moments before.

Momma was only a few blocks away, so I started going over there a couple of times a day. We'd taken the keys to her car, worried she'd get lost or cause an accident. After a while she got to a point where she needed so much care, going over once or twice a day wasn't enough. I had to make sure she was eating and taking her medications several times a day. I hesitated to move her out of her house. It was her sanctuary. It was an expression of who she was and what she did for most of her adult life. Coming in the front door, the first thing you'd see was a huge sculpture of Black Jesus. When you sat down on the couch, you'd face pictures of Martin Luther King Jr., Malcolm X, and Nelson Mandela. These heroes kept her going. But a little at a time, we moved her into the extra bedroom in our house. A couple of nights a week, I'd have the bus from senior day care bring her to our house. After dinner, we'd delay taking her home until it was too late, so we'd suggest she stay the night. Eventually, she just stayed with us full time.

Momma was happy living with us. She loved seeing the grandchildren when they'd come over after school. When it was quiet, she watched television on the living room couch, and played solitaire with a deck of 18 worn-out cards. One of those times when Kim was in town, she brought Momma a new deck of playing cards. Momma wouldn't play with them until we messed them up a little. She didn't like how the new ones were slippery, and she really didn't need 52 cards.

Although Momma had a hard time understanding some things, she knew what I was up to with the Carrier land. She would cheer me on when I was on the phone, or giggle about my "good trouble."

Having Momma living with us was good for me too. When I was growing up, Momma was a politician who was well-known in the community and always busy trying to solve other people's problems. The hardest part about this was sharing her with so many people. Even though I knew what she did and why she did it, we had to give up so much of our time with her to strangers. She hardly slept or watched TV, and she didn't have a social life. Every day was centered around protecting people's rights and waiting on the next phone call. As a child, I was jealous. So this time with her was precious to me, even if she wasn't completely aware all the time.

I had plenty to keep me busy during this time but the lawsuit was always on my mind. I checked in with Karen every so often to see whether she'd heard from the court about how the judge planned to conduct the proceeding.

In early July 2019, Karen told me she'd been out to the Carrier land. She checked the mailbox at the property and found a small piece of paper that looked like evidence that there was still drilling going on at the property. We already knew there was still drilling going on because the pumpjack was still operating, but the ticket Karen found had important information on it. It showed that on July 4, 2019, an oil truck had picked up 160 barrels of crude from an "active well." Chevron had told the court that there was only a dry well in the area. It showed the operator was Pay Ventures LLC, a company in Carencro, Louisiana. The well was identified as "Bernard 01." Consistent with what my granddaddy suspected, the ticket showed that the oil was being removed from the land in the middle of the night: the time on the ticket was 2:35 am.

Then, on July 23, 2019, Karen got an email from Wilson with an attachment called "Reason for Judgment" issued by Judge Sigur 13 days before, on July 10, 2019. Maybe I shouldn't have been, but I was shocked when I read it.

The document said the family's claim against the defendants was barred by the legal principle called "prescription," meaning the family had waited too long to file the lawsuit. The judge's decision didn't address numerous issues raised in the original complaint, for example, our claim that Chevron/Texaco was still drilling on our land. Even if the Carriers were barred from suing for allegations in previous years, we had the right to sue for what had happened in recent years and in future years, including the environmental damage to the land caused by the drilling.

The document also didn't address the failure of the Duhe family to respond to the complaint or make an appearance at the hearing. The Reason for Judgment didn't address our request for discovery, which would provide the family with the opportunity to make the case that prescription didn't apply in our case, even though the judge ruled at the hearing that the Carriers were entitled to conduct discovery.

Karen texted our family that day, saying, "Well, family. We lost."

Karen's text was strange because the Reason for Judgment didn't dismiss the case or close it. It had some analysis of the case but it wasn't obvious at that point that we'd lost. For that reason, I couldn't understand why she would say "We lost" unless someone else told her that.

The document seemed strange for another reason. I was told that in Louisiana, a "Reason for Judgment" is normally issued only after the issuance of a "Final Judgment," which the judge had not issued in the Carrier case. So the judge's decision to issue a "Reason for Judgment" at that point was not usual procedure.

Neither of the Carriers' attorneys filed in opposition to the Reason for Judgment or formally ask about its significance. Karen would later tell me Wilson had contacted her to say the "Reason for Judgment" was an order dismissing the case and that the family's chances of prevailing in an appeal were small.

About a week after the judge issued the "Reason for Judgment," Chevron filed a "Proposed Judgment," which, if the judge adopted it, would dismiss the case. Again, our attorneys filed nothing in response.

At around the same time, Judge Sigur got involved in the case in an unusual way. I sent Karen a text one morning saying I wanted to talk to her about the dismissal of the case. Karen responded a few minutes later. She said she couldn't talk because she was on a conference call with Judge Sigur and some of her family members. I was surprised since this could be an inappropriate ex parte communication. Parties aren't normally permitted to speak with a judge assigned to their case unless the other parties are present. I couldn't imagine why Karen and some of the family were talking to the judge. Karen was so open with me about it, I thought she probably didn't understand the impropriety of what they were doing.

I called Karen later that day and asked her why she was on the phone with the judge. She was vague and I couldn't make sense of her response. Later I texted her to say I was troubled she hadn't invited me to be a part of that phone call with the judge. Karen texted me back and said "That call wasn't about Carrier business." I couldn't think of why else there would be a conference call between several family members and the judge assigned to our lawsuit while the case was still pending. The only thing I could think of was that someone in the family knew him personally. The Black community here is small and close. Judge Sigur was Black and well-known. But it apparently wasn't that: later Karen told me the judge advised the family on that conference call that they shouldn't appeal the case because we'd lose.

On August 23, 2019, Judge Sigur issued a "Final Judgment," dismissing the family's case. It said the dismissal was "with prejudice," meaning the matter could never be raised again in the parish court.

The procedures in this case continued to be unusual. Almost a month after the issued a Final Judgment, the

Duhe family — defendants in the lawsuit — submitted a letter to the court objecting to our claims. This was the first document the Duhes submitted to the court since we filed the lawsuit. The letter should not have been a part of the court's record and, to me at least, the late notice was an admission that the Duhes were in default. If the Duhes didn't sense some risk or culpability, I doubted they would have bothered to draw attention to the fact that they never officially objected to our claims. The court didn't acknowledge the letter in any way as far as I knew.

All of this felt wrong. My family hadn't had its day in court — only a 20-minute hearing where we weren't permitted to put on our case. Our lawyers hadn't been advocating for us in spite of all the unusual circumstances, including how the judge ignored his own ruling on discovery. I didn't believe the judge could be confident of his legal analysis without understanding the facts in the case. I didn't understand how Karen could give up so easily.

The effects of this judgment on my family were bad enough. Applying "prescription" to our case could also set a terrible precedent for other cases. The Carriers weren't the only family in Iberia Parish to have lost land or oil resources in past years. Like my family, many would not have known how to prove what they suspected. They might not have known how to find documents or a lawyer to help them. They might lose jobs for trying. For a long time, a Black man in Louisiana could be lynched for "insolence." I imagine challenging the rights of powerful whites in rural Louisiana might be considered by some as insolent.

27

THE TRANSCRIPT

The next thing on my list was to get a hold the transcript documenting what happened at the April hearing. It just didn't seem the judge's decision was supported by what happened in that hearing.

But I didn't get to this for a while. I couldn't face it. I tried not to think about the litigation and I tried to distract myself with the other things in my life. I didn't talk to anyone about it for weeks. But I decided to try to figure out a way to appeal. I knew I'd need to do a lot of work in less than two months to find an appellate lawyer and prepare for the filing. The appeal deadline would be 67 days after the Final Judgment was signed. I finally found the Final Judgment in the courthouse files, which was signed on August 23, 2019.

I'd also need the hearing "extract" and transcript to provide clues about how and whether the court had committed legal error in dismissing the case. An extract is a summary of the hearing that is routinely produced for the record of a proceeding, normally within a few days. The transcript is a word-for-word report and, in Iberia Parish, it's only created if a party requests it. The extract wasn't in the court's on-line files, but it hadn't been posted. This seemed strange since the hearing had been held five months before.

Because I wasn't confident the Court would be responsive to my request for a copy of the extract or hearing transcript, Kim ordered a copy of each. She got the extract immediately from the Clerk of Court's office, but we knew it would take weeks for the transcript to arrive because the reporter had to create it rather than just copy it. Apparently, none of the attorneys on either side thought the transcript was important enough to order.

After that, we'd have to push to get that transcript. Even after we'd ordered a copy, Kim had to make several phone calls and send several emails to the court reporter and the court administrator. At first, the office said they couldn't locate the audio tape. Then the reporter was in a trial. The reporter finally called to say the paper copy was ready for pick up in the judge's office. Kim had left town by then, so I sent my daughter, Tamika, to pick it up in the judge's office because no one knew her there.

That night, I laid in bed reading the transcript. I was confused. Some of what was in the transcript didn't match up with what I remembered from the short hearing. Maybe I wasn't remembering everything as it happened. I waited until a paper copy was included in the court's official case file and then sent a text to the court clerk to suggest he might want to compare the audio tape of the April 8 hearing with the certified transcript.

The court clerk was a Republican who was elected in a landslide vote after the previous court clerk, Mike Thibodeaux, went to prison in July 2019. Thibodeaux was convicted of 14 counts of racketeering, theft, maintaining false records, perjury and malfeasance – all related to his position as court clerk. So there had been a lot of problems in that courthouse when the court clerk took office.

On the other hand, I knew the court clerk and I trusted him.

The transcript from the Carrier hearing and my inquiry to the court clerk seemed to be related to another controversy related to a dispute between the Parish Court's Chief Judge Lori Landry, and the District Attorney Bo Duhe. The same Bo Duhe.[32]

Judge Landry grew up in the West End in a family of respected public officials. She was the first Black woman appointed to the DA's office in New Iberia. Bo Duhe was her boss. The Bo Duhe whose family was a named defendant in the Carrier lawsuit. Later, Judge Landry was elected to the parish bench. She was open about her view that the DA's office prosecuted and settled criminal cases differently, depending on whether the defendant was Black or white. Duhe's office apparently wanted to use her statements against her. He directed his staff file to motions for Judge Landry's recusal in 300 criminal cases, claiming she was biased against the prosecution.[33]

After a lot of procedural wrangling between Landry and the DA's office, the Louisiana Supreme Court appointed retired Louisiana judge, Harry Randow, to conduct a public hearing to consider the DA's recusal motions.

On the day of the hearing, the courtroom was packed with mostly Black residents who showed up to express their support for Judge Landry. A couple of assistant DA's testified against her. One testified that Judge Landry threatened her during a trial. Judge Landry was known for her expressive style, but not as a person who was threatening, and no one doubted her intellect or legal acumen. After the testimony, Judge Randow stated he would need to hear the audio tapes of the hearings during which Judge Landry had allegedly made prejudicial or threatening statements. The judge had the transcripts, but he apparently didn't want to rely on them exclusively. The assistant DA representing the office objected and was overruled.

The crowd in the courtroom waited for hours while Landry, members of the DA's office, and Judge Randow convened behind closed doors to listen to the tapes.

When they returned to the courtroom, Judge Randow announced that the DA's office would withdraw all motions "with prejudice" (meaning, they could not be renewed in the future). There wasn't any explanation for why Duhe would, after months of attacks on Landry, abruptly withdraw the recusal motions.

In his public statement, Duhe said, "It's in the best interest of the community to put this aside."[34]

After learning about what might have been falsified transcripts and testimony in Judge Landry's hearing, Kim and I tried to get a copy of the audio and the stenotype tape from Judge Sigur's hearing in our lawsuit. On one of the requests, the court administrator copied Judge Louis Pittman, the same Louis Pittman who had for years represented Glen Mayo, and gave the abstract to the Tax Assessor's office showing a quarter of Carrier land belonged to Mayo. Our request for the audio and the stenotype tape was denied.

There seemed to be an unusual amount of drama involving audiotapes and transcripts.

28

A CONTRACT

IF I WAS GOING TO keep going with the litigation, I needed a copy of the abstract that Craig Stewart had hired a consultant, Lisa Broussard, to create. I believed the Broussard abstract, combined with the abstract I'd gotten from the tax assessor's office, would be useful evidence if our case ever went to trial; and help us fend off more challenges to the ownership of our land, such as those that seemed to be facilitated by the tax assessor's office.

I stuck to my usual practice of just showing up rather than providing advance notice to anyone who might want to cover their tracks or avoid me. I knew Lisa well enough to believe she was trustworthy, but I didn't know what she'd been doing for the previous many years. So, without any advance notice, Kim and I drove to Lisa's ranch near Youngsville, about 15 miles from New Iberia. When I pulled into the gravel drive, Lisa approached the car with a small pack of barking dogs. She was middle-aged, wiry, one of those women who looks elegant in blue jeans. Lisa recognized me and said she was glad to see me. After I told her why I was there, Lisa explained that she'd completed work on the abstract. She never gave it to our lawyer because he'd never paid her for it.

"I understand," I said. "Is the abstract still available?" I chose my words carefully, hoping I wouldn't have to come up with the $4,000 we'd owed her for the past ten years.

"Yeah, sure," she said. "I have it on a CD. You can have it. You know, there were lots of strange documents I found involving the Carrier property."

I felt relieved about this last disclosure because I felt more confident about the work she'd done. Lisa was related to one of the people I believed had filed one of those strange documents. She said something indirectly that I interpreted as a reference to it. I didn't respond. Kim seemed ready to jump in, but stayed quiet.

That evening after I got home, I downloaded the files from the CD Lisa had given me and went through the list of documents on it. I compared Lisa's abstract to those I'd found in the courthouse, the Romero abstract, and the tax assessor's list. It was all familiar to me and what I expected, except for one shocking thing.

Lisa found a document that no one else had. It was a contract dated 1978 between Chevron and Karen's mother, Shirley May, the daughter of my daddy's sister,

Beatrice. The contract granted Chevron the right to drill on the Carrier land and granted the royalties to Shirley May. Because no one else had so far found this contract, I assumed it had been removed from the courthouse file room at some point.

The contract between Chevron and Shirley May seemed like proof Chevron knew the land belonged to the Carriers. If we'd had a copy of this contract a year before, everything might have worked out differently because Chevron could not have denied the existence of the well or the ownership of the Carrier land.

The contract was significant for other reasons. Chevron surely knew about it and could have used it as leverage to convince Karen to drop the lawsuit. Whether or not Chevron used its leverage, Karen's side of the family probably wouldn't have wanted it to be disclosed. As far as I knew, Shirley May never told the other family members who shared ownership of the land that she was profiting from the resources on the family land. At the time, the land was owned by ten family members who had equal rights to any income from it. The contract could have been evidence that something illegal had occurred.

The disclosure of the contract might have caused a lot of stress among family members, but I didn't think it could have hurt our lawsuit. Shirley May had no proof that she owned the land or authority to sign a contract on behalf of the family. For that reason, as Chevron would know, the contract wasn't legal when it was signed.

If Mayo and Wilson knew about the contract, they could have used it to convince Karen to abandon the lawsuit. Of course, I didn't know the whole truth of it. I only knew what it looked like. I'd learned to speculate.

29

THE FOURTH LAWYER

Momma always said "Being a Carrier is a blessing and a curse." By this time, I was wondering what the blessing part was. I was in shock after Judge Sigur's dismissal of our case, and normally I would have spent some time building back my confidence and re-centering myself before I made any decisions. But I didn't know enough about legal processes to know what doors might close if I didn't do something soon. I talked to Kim about whether my family should appeal. There were a lot of obstacles standing in the way; some we knew about and some we didn't.

My first challenge was going to be lawyers. I couldn't trust the lawyers who filed the original complaint, and finding another one would be difficult. The facts of the case were complicated, and in Louisiana, most lawyers with the kind of expertise we needed had clients in the oil and gas industry.

Then there was the money. Our trial attorneys took our lawsuit on a contingency fee basis, meaning they'd get a share of any money awarded in the lawsuit. But appellate attorneys didn't operate like that. They required payment upfront because there were no prospects of monetary awards from a successful appeal. I didn't have the $15,000 I needed to pay for an attorney and the court fees.

Getting over these hurdles, however, wouldn't make a bit of difference if I couldn't convince Karen to step down as administrator. For as long as the court identified her in that role, no one else could file an appeal. She'd already been very clear that she had no interest in pursuing an appeal, but she wouldn't tell me why. Maybe Karen was threatened or paid to walk away from the lawsuit. Maybe she was just exhausted. I asked myself many times whether I had the strength to start the fight all over again. Even if the appellate court found in our favor, that would only be putting us back at the starting line.

I thought about my granddaddy and decided I wasn't ready to give up. If nothing else, the process would expose more of the truth. I would just take it one day at a time. I had my faith and I knew that would get me through.

The first thing we had to do was file a Notice of Appeal with the Third Circuit Court in Lake Charles. This just stated our intent to file an appeal without a commitment to do anything.

Kim was trying to find an attorney who had appellate experience and didn't have clients in the oil and gas industry. A friend in Lafayette told Kim about an attorney named Gabe Duhon in Abbeville about 20 miles west of New Iberia in Vermilion Parish.

Even before we met him, Gabe seemed to be the perfect person for the case. He didn't work with oil and gas companies, but had the expertise we needed. He'd been a "landman" in the oil and gas industry before he became a private attorney. Landmen negotiate oil and gas leases with landowners, manage the planning process, inspect surfaces before drilling. They know about regulations and land maps and contracts. Gabe would understand the evidence supporting the Carriers' lawsuit, its significance, and how to use it. He knew the risks he would take with the case and he knew the potential rewards.

A friend joined me for my first meeting with Gabe. Gabe's office was across from the Vermillion Parish Courthouse in a small store front. His receptionist sat in a room behind a window instead of at a desk in the reception area. Maybe the office had once been a medical or dental office. Gabe was middle-aged, balding with a beard. He had a stern look but was friendly and outgoing when we met with him. We spent more than an hour talking about the lawsuit and the significance of some of our documents. Gabe replied with headshaking and some profanity. I recall he referred to our previous lawyers as "motherfuckers." He seemed to know exactly what happened and how to interpret the documents I showed him.

A few weeks after our meeting, I got a loan for Gabe's fees and signed a contract engaging his services. Having a good lawyer was just the beginning. Getting to the point where the Carriers could submit an appellate brief to the court was another. It was going to be one thing after another.

30

CHANGING THE ADMINISTRATOR

Before I could file the appeal, I needed to be assigned as administrator because Karen didn't want to go any further in the case. I needed to ask Karen to step down. I sent her a text shortly after our meeting with Gabe. I said I wanted to appeal the judge's decision. She sent me a text back, calling me a "troublemaker" and telling me to let it go.

I couldn't let it go. I kept thinking about my granddaddy working in the sugarcane on his own land for pennies a day. My daddy wanted me to find justice. I asked Karen whether the family could have a conference call or meeting to discuss the case. She said she wouldn't agree to any meetings or give me contact information for the landowners on her side of the family.

I waited a week or so and then sent Karen a text asking whether she would sign an affidavit that would permit me to take over the administrator role. Karen said she was in Florida and would be home in a few days. She'd sign an affidavit if I brought a lawyer and a notary to her house in Gray, about 80 miles east of New Iberia.

One Sunday after Karen returned from Florida, Ray, my daughter Tamika, and I drove to Karen's house. A lawyer friend joined us because Karen had said she'd sign the affidavit if a lawyer was present. We set out that day without providing Karen any advance notice. I worried Karen would have second thoughts if she knew we were coming.

Driving to Karen's house reminded me of my family's drives to Karen's family house on Sundays. We loved those drives and I was sad that this one wasn't going to take us to a happy family dinner or playing in the yard. But I was enjoying myself too in a way. I felt like something bigger was with us. I said, "We go by spiritual guidance – something was telling me today is the day."

As we approached Karen's house, I suggested Ray slow down to see whether the family was home and whether they might have company. Everyone waited in the car while I went to the door. The blinds were open so I knew Karen saw us coming up the driveway, and she knew we saw her.

"Hey Cuz Karen," I yelled as I approached the house. I was smiling when Karen came out of the house and, after we all said some awkward hellos, I introduced my lawyer friend to Karen. "She's a notary," I said, "so we can sign the papers."

Karen replied, " I said I would sign them if you got an attorney to draw up the papers."

"My friend is an attorney and a notary. She drew up the papers for us"

Karen was breathing hard and her eyes weren't meeting mine, like she wasn't sure what to do next. I told her I wanted her to read the papers before she signed them. I didn't want her saying later she didn't know what she was signing.

She looked over the papers and then everybody signed them. After that, Karen called our Uncle Smithy. Uncle Smithy is not really my uncle but my daddy's nephew on Karen's side of the family. We call him "Uncle" because he's a little older and one of those people who feels like an uncle. We needed his signature too, because he was on the court records as co-administrator. Karen had told me not to talk to Uncle Smithy about the appeal, but I called him in advance and he agreed the family should appeal. I hated all this sneaking around, but I was trying to do the right in for the family.

Karen told us Uncle Smithy was home, and we set out for his house in Patterson, about 35 miles in the direction of New Iberia.

We weren't ten minutes down the road before Karen texted my cell. When I heard the phone beep, I was thinking "I am not even going to look at that." Karen's text said "take a picture of the document and send it to me." We'd told Karen we would mail a copy to her, but I guessed Karen couldn't wait that long. I wondered whether she'd already talked to someone, maybe Tregg Wilson and Keith Mayo, or Judge Sigur.

When we arrived at Uncle Smithy's, he was watching the football game. I'm a big Saints fan too, so I knew he was in a hurry to get back to the game. At the door, he greeted us with a smile. We sat and watched the game for a few minutes and Uncle Smithy said he was glad about what I was doing. He said "Let me get my glasses." and then read read the papers and signed them. He winked at me. We got back in the car feeling like we'd just won the lottery.

On the way home, Karen called me several times. I didn't answer the phone. I just didn't want anything to interrupt this moment of clarity about what I was going to do. We stopped for fried chicken and made an evening of it.

The next morning, I went to the courthouse to file the petition for a change in administration with our affidavits and our feelings of excitement. We arrived when the offices opened at 8 am. Normally, we would have filed the petition for the change in administration and left. But we knew the judge on duty that day would have to sign our petition to make it official. We also knew there was mischief in parts of that courthouse. I could just imagine the petition getting lost or delayed so that we couldn't meet the deadline. I didn't want to give anyone a chance to sabotage what we were doing, so we waited to get the signature of the judge on duty.

After about an hour, the judge on duty came out of his chambers. When he did, I could feel my heart pounding a little. Maybe he would challenge the filing or refuse to sign it.

The Judge read the document and signed it without any comment. He glanced at us and turned away as if to say, "This is not my problem." Julie, the court clerk's assistant, took the papers and called upstairs to see how much to charge me for the filing. She told someone on the phone the number of the case. Julie's microphone was on so I heard the woman on the other end of the line say, "Wait, I am coming down to see the document." Julie made a funny face at the phone. A few minutes later, a woman came down the stairs and took the document from Julie. I didn't know who she was, but she looked at us like she knew us. We left feeling relieved that job was behind us.

On October 19, 2019, Karen sent me a text: "Hilliard (Uncle Smithy's real name) and I are done with this Administration, it's back in ur hands, sugarcane and whatever we're good in St. Mary (parish) and I'm good in Terrebonne (parish)." I didn't know what to think, but I felt alone.

31

GETTING THE FILES

Once I became the administrator, I needed to get the files from the attorneys, Mayo and Wilson. As administrator, I was entitled to them. Normally, it would have been a routine transaction to get the files from the two attorneys who had been representing us. But nothing was routine about this case so far.

I called Tregg Wilson's office on October 22 and told his secretary I wanted to pick up the case files. Wilson was in court, but called me back a few minutes later. I told him I was the administrator for the lawsuit and needed the case files. He said he wasn't in the office and suggested I could pick up the files on Thursday because he'd be in court on Wednesday.

I didn't know why he needed to be there since I just wanted to pick up the files, but I didn't say anything.

I didn't ask him about the appeal, but Wilson said we were too late to file one, that the date for filing had passed.

"I told Karen it's too late and everything is finished," he said.

I asked him, "Are you telling me it's too late?"

After he said "Yes," I asked him again, "Are you telling me it's too late?"

And after he said yes, I asked him again, "Are you telling me it's too late?"

"Am I being recorded? You keep asking me the same thing over and over." I told him I was trying to listen to my momma talking at the same time.

I drove to Wilson's Baton Rouge office the next day, Wednesday, with my lawyer friend. We weren't going to wait until Thursday. That would have given him time for mischief.

Wilson's office was along a highway, outside of the main part of the city. It wasn't much, sitting next to an unpaved parking lot and the back of some condominiums. When we arrived and I got out of the car, my spirit was not feeling right about something. I prepared my mind for trouble.

The secretary was not at the front desk. Wilson walked out of a door down the hall. I think he was surprised to see us. He forgot to say hello..

"We had an agreement you were coming tomorrow," he said. He was kind of half-smiling.

Before I could reply, my lawyer spoke. "As Robby's lawyer, I had to come with her and I have a doctor appointment tomorrow."

Then Wilson looked at me and asked, "What do you need the file for?" It was none of his business at this point. The files didn't belong to him.

But I told him we intended to file an appeal.

He said, now for the fourth time, "It's too late for an appeal. I already spoke with Karen about that." My lawyer friend began to explain to him why the deadline to file an appeal hadn't passed. Before she could finish, he interrupted and agreed that the appeal date hadn't passed. Right there, he admitted to his client and an attorney that he had lied.

I saw our case file on top of the secretary's desk and wondered why it was sitting out there in the open. I suspected Wilson had invited Karen to pick up the file that day, so I'd never see it. Maybe that's why he seemed so nervous.

I noticed something else that was suspicious. On top of the file folders was a letter addressed to Karen dated July 23, five days before the judge's decision was published. The letter informed Karen that it was too late to appeal. The letter was signed in ink, so it was an original that had never been mailed. Attached to it was a sticker used for certified mail that hadn't been filled out. I wondered whether the letter had been typed that day and would have been mailed if we hadn't arrived in Wilson's office a day early. It seemed Wilson had become part of the Texas team.

I went through the files after getting home later that day and I found another interesting document. It was a draft of the original complaint to the court. It was very different from the one Wilson filed. It clearly stated what had happened on the Carrier land. It used words like "conspiracy," "fraud," and "theft." Unlike the complaint that had been filed, the draft complaint in the file would have been clear to a 12-year-old – or any reporter. Apparently, this was the draft complaint we authorized Keith Mayo to file, and then someone wrote a complaint that was obscure and incomplete, which was the one that was filed. The file also included printed copies of Kim's blog posting describing our case. Apparently, they were being diligent, although toward what end I wasn't sure at this point.[35]

There was what I would call a little panic that night around midnight. Wilson texted me to say he was no longer representing the family. "After you left with the file yesterday, Mr. Duhon contacted me via email asking me to file a Notice of Appeal. I am not filing a Notice of Appeal in this case....and I'm not representing you as the administratrix in the succession.[36] You did not give me any notice that you were seeking that appointment and we've had no discussion about you engaging me to represent you as administratrix – and I'm not interested in undertaking such representation. You have spoken with (two attorneys) – if you want representation then go sign a contract with one of them. I am no longer involved as I have spoken with Karen May and she understands that I am no longer representing the Succession in either case in this matter. So, as per our conversation you have told me that you are aware of the deadlines for appeal – please be aware that you make arrangements to handle any appeal either on your own or through your attorney (in any event, as we discussed yesterday, I will not be handling this matter going forward.")

Lying in bed, there in my pajamas, I giggled. Wilson texting me at midnight with such a rambling, inarticulate message. He knew that the moment I became administrator, I became his client because he was engaged to represent the family (the succession as he referred to it) because they were the plaintiffs, not Karen or me. Karen was only the person assigned to represent the family. If that representative were to change, he still had a responsibility to represent the clients in the case. Of course, I didn't want him working on it anyway.

The next day, Gabe called to tell me Karen had called him the day before. Gabe's assistant answered the call and then privately told Gabe that Karen was on the phone. He privately asked her to take a message, then stood next to her recording the phone conversation. Gabe's assistant asked Karen whether she wanted to leave a message. Karen didn't hold back. She said Gabe had no authorization to represent the Carriers in the lawsuit because she had not engaged him. Karen suggested she had been tricked into signing an affidavit transferring the role of administrator to me. She claimed that she retained that role, and that I had taken the case files from Wilson's office without authority.

In a letter to Gabe a couple of weeks later, Wilson refused to withdraw as attorney of record even though he still refused to represent the family. Apparently, he owed a large sum in filing fees to the parish court, and would have to pay them if he withdrew. Once again, Wilson was putting a lot of questionable stuff in writing.

During this same period, I tried to get the rest of the case files from Keith Mayo in Texas because what Wilson gave me wasn't complete. The files that were in Mayo's office included original maps of the land and the contract Karen signed when she engaged Mayo's firm. In September, and then again in October, I sent Mayo several emails requesting the case files. After received no response by November, I sent a certified letter to each of Mayo's three Texas addresses. I knew he got the letter because I received a return receipt from one of the addresses.

Later, I asked Gabe to ask Mayo for the case files. Shortly after that, Gabe sent a sternly-worded email to Mayo, threatening to sue him if he didn't turn over the files. Mayo promised to send them by overnight mail that week. They never arrived.

32

THE NOTICE OF APPEAL

In late October 2019, I filed the "Notice of Appeal." Again, this wasn't the appeal — just a filing to alert the court and the parties that we'd be filing an appeal. The court accepted the filing and would set a briefing date later in the process. Because the parish courthouse had previously denied our request for the audiotapes of the hearing, our Notice of Appeal to the higher court formally asked for copies of the audiotapes, which it would have to get from the lower court. We wanted to make sure the hearing transcript was accurate.

A few days after our filing, I texted Karen to let her know I'd filed the Notice of Appeal. I said I wanted to talk to her about it. I thought she'd want to know the legal issues we would address and Gabe's assessment of the case. I was ready to tell her I got the $12,000 we needed to retain the lawyers and pay the court fees.[37] She didn't call me back. She replied with a text that asked one thing:

"Do you think the court will investigate Judge Sigur?"

I wasn't expecting that answer. I mean, I was truly surprised that an investigation of Judge Sigur was the only thing on Karen's mind. Maybe she thought Judge Sigur had done something wrong. I suspected he had.

I didn't answer her question.

33

THE TAX ASSESSOR AGAIN

I DON'T KNOW WHAT HE was getting out of it, but New Iberia's tax assessor, Ricky Huval, was still doing things that created the impression he was trying to give away Carrier land. In November, after I filed the Notice of Appeal, I checked the tax assessor's website. This time, it showed that the Romero family owned almost half of the Carrier land. To make this change, the tax assessor would have had to ignore official abstracts and the 2006 court order, and he couldn't have had any other official document to justify the change in ownership. There wasn't one.

I decided to confront him and asked Kim to join me in a meeting with him on November 18, 2019. The tax assessor's office was in a small government building across from the parish courthouse. I went to Huval's office without an appointment because, if I'd asked for one, I guessed Huval would have found a way to avoid me or cover his tracks. The receptionist greeted me warmly and invited us into Huval's office. We sat down in chairs facing Huval's desk. It was a modest office, not a place you'd expect someone to have the power to mess with the parish's most important resource and the lives of parish residents.

The last time I'd met with Huval was in an unpleasant meeting 14 years before, but he greeted me like we were old friends. "Hi Robby, so nice to see you again. What can I do for you?" He was breathing hard and hitting the keys on his computer. I waited until he looked up.

"Mr. Huval, I came to ask you why the tax assessor records show that 75% of the Carrier land belongs to the Romero family." I was trying to speak slowly so I'd stay calm. Huval began by saying he made the changes "according to a court order."

"I'd like to see the court order, please. No one in my family has seen any official documents transferring my family's property."

Then I added, "You should know there is pending litigation."

Huval punched a few keys on his desktop computer and then called in one of his staff. A few minutes later a tall, very young man walked in with a sheet of paper. He was flushed. Kim smiled and said hello to him, and I tried to catch his eye, but he looked down. Huval looked at the paper and changed his story.

"We made these changes on the basis of an audit." He handed me a piece of paper he'd printed out from the assessor's public website. It was another abstract, listing all of the official documents associated with the land. Huval said, "This shows you how we justified a change in property ownership."

I reminded him that I had a court order affirming my family's continuous ownership of the land and asked him several times which documents he relied upon to effectively overturn a court document. He didn't respond.

"Whatever they are," I said, "they can't be legal."

Huval didn't hesitate. "I don't care whether they're legal or not."[38]

I asked what motivated the office to conduct an audit of the Carrier property. Huval said he changed the ownership shares at the request of Glen Romero. He said he wouldn't change them back.

I looked at the abstract Huval had given me and saw two documents listed that I'd never seen on any other abstract or anywhere else.

During this conversation, Huval addressed Kim as "Babe." The first time he said it, I could feel her breathing change and I was laughing inside. The second time he said it, she interrupted him.

"Excuse me, Mr. Huval" she said, "you may not address me as 'Babe.'"

He fumbled. "I meant nothing by it." I kept a straight face and told him I planned to pay the taxes on the property as my family always had.

Huval wrapped up our meeting by saying, "I hope you know I'm not mad at you." For what? Trying to claim my family's property? Did he think I cared about whether he was mad at me? I didn't respond.

We stood up and walked out of Huval's office. I was exhausted. I'd been fighting the same fight for more than 20 years, each fight a variation of the last one, each one emotionally draining.

When we went outside, the sun was bright and hot. Kim said she wanted to go to the courthouse files to investigate the two unfamiliar documents on that abstract Huval gave us. I was glad I couldn't join her right then.

"I have to go get Momma now from daycare," I said. I could tell my voice was shaking. Kim looked at the abstract Huval gave me, and wrote down the information about the two documents. She gave me a quick hug. She called later to tell me what she found in the courthouse files.

"When I walked into the office," she said, "the receptionist winked at me and held out her hand in the direction of the door to the file room. I felt like I belonged,"

She found the two documents listed in abstract, but they weren't relevant to the Carrier land. The first document was in the binder where the abstract said it would be. It was a will bequeathing a plot of parish farmland to a grandchild. None of the names were familiar, certainly not "Romero." The document identified the land as comprising 23 acres, but the survey numbers were not those assigned to the Carrier land. The second document was a will signed by one of Romero's family members, bequeathing an unidentified property she didn't own to her children, none of whom were Glen or Mayo Romero. Neither were official documents and neither would have motivated an honest tax assessor to change the ownership of Carrier land. I later checked the information at the tax assessor's website. None of the documents associated with the Carrier land showed a transfer of the property to anyone.

A few days later, I sent Huval a certified letter describing the relevant parts of our conversation with him. The letter asked for an official explanation of his audit results and threatened an appeal through the courts if he didn't reply by December 15, 2019. Although I received a signed receipt indicating the letter had been received, Huval's office never responded to the letter. This seemed like an admission of Huval's culpability and I learned a little more about how people like me can lose their land. I doubted I would ever follow up on my threat of litigation, but at least I had a record of my objection to how he'd changed the abstract and the tax assessor files. The whole thing angered me, but it didn't worry me. Huval's audit results were obviously wrong, and I continued paying the taxes on the whole 23 acres.

I learned later I wasn't the only who had problems with the way Huval managed his operation. In 2018, an online newspaper reported that Huval increased the taxable value of the property of the Iberia Parish Clerk of Court — at the time, Michael Thibodeaux — shortly after Thibodeaux fired Huval's son, Ryan. The paper said Huval's daughter worked for District Attorney Bo Duhe, who subsequently indicted Thibodeaux following an audit of the Clerk of Court's operation. This is where I live.[39]

34

LEGAL PROCEDURES

WITH EVERY STEP OF THIS lawsuit, there was something to be nervous about. This time it was waiting for the official case file the parish court was required to send to the appellate court for its review. The Parish court had 45 days to submit it from the date I paid the court fees in December 2019.

I waited until mid-January to call the Parish court clerk's office to find out whether the official case file had been transmitted to the appellate court. The woman who answered the phone responded that there had been a delay because the court reporter hadn't provided a certified copy of the transcript. I was surprised the court clerk's office would share this information with me, and interpreted this confidence as a show of support. But also, this made no sense. More than a year before, the court sent us a certified copy of that transcript and confirmed that a copy of it was in the court's case file. Now, according to the court clerk's office, the reporter was holding up the transmittal of the court's official files because she needed to provide a certified transcript. This seemed to confirm my belief that parts of the transcript had been falsified. If the transcript had been authentic, the reporter only needed to copy it and stamp it. Maybe it was all just an honest mistake, but I hadn't seen an honest mistake in this litigation so far.

The parish court submitted the official case file to the 3rd Circuit Court on time. It included two interesting documents. The transcript presented to the court was not certified. Apparently, the court reporter refused to certify the transcript. This seemed like an admission that the transcript didn't match the audiotape. The court reporter could lose her job and even her license if she was involved in falsifying her work products. But the damage was done. The court reporter's certification stamp was on my copy of the transcript, and I had an email from the court administrator, copied to the court reporter, assuring me the transcript was authentic.

The other interesting document in the file sent to the Court was a letter from the court clerk, when the court clerk took office, stating he had tried unsuccessfully to get a certified copy of the transcript. He seemed to be distancing himself from the court reporter, and whoever directed the court reporter to certify a falsified copy of the transcript.

In February, after receiving the official case file, Gabe filed a motion asking the 3rd Circuit Court (the appellate court) to order the 16th JDC (the Iberia Parish court) to provide the audiotape from the April 2019 hearing. The appellate court granted the motion and ordered the 16th JDC to provide "all" audiotapes from the hearing in their "unadulterated" form.

The court didn't get the tapes from the 16th JDC for several months, and finally shared them with Gabe in early July. The court gave Gabe a couple of extra weeks to file his appellate brief so he'd have time to review the tapes and compare them to the transcript. He met with me a few days before the appellate brief was due so we could review the draft appellate brief and hear a portion of the audiotape.

Gabe left the room after turning on the audiotape. I didn't understand why he wasn't there to consult with me about what was on the audiotape and whether it matched the transcript. He didn't give me a copy of the transcript and I didn't have a copy with me, so I wasn't sure whether what I heard on the tape was complete and accurate. Someone told me later that if the audiotapes didn't match the transcript, the court might have directed Gabe to keep that information from anyone, including his own client, during an investigation. With that, I let it go. I wanted to let Gabe do his job. I trusted him.

On July 27, 2020, Gabe filed the appellate brief with the 3rd Circuit (appellate court). The brief made three key points. First, it argued that the court erred in dismissing the case on the basis of prescription. The court did not have adequate facts for such a ruling and misapplied the principle of law. Second, it argued that the court erred by failing to recognize the Carriers' claim that the oil drilling was ongoing, so that the application of prescription was irrelevant for recent extraction activity, even if it could be applied to activity in earlier years. Third, it argued the court erred by failing to find the Duhe family in default when it dismissed the case. Dismissing the case "with prejudice" meant the Duhes would never have to respond to the allegations.

I was so relieved to get to that point. For almost 20 years, I'd put up with nonsense and betrayals, incompetent lawyers, government officials, and what looked like falsified documents. If the court found in my favor, I would be able to tell my family's story for the first time, with evidence and oaths and someone to listen to the truth. That's all I really wanted. A place to tell the truth.

And like I said, it was a turning point in my life to get my granddaddy to the appellate court. He was being acknowledged in a court that never would have been accessible to him during his life. His name was on a document that asserted his rights. Nothing would be the same after filing that appeal, although, at the time, I didn't know what would change.

A couple of days later, four of the five defendants filed a motion for an extension of time to file their reply brief. The party who was not included as a signatory to the motion was the Duhe family. Again, the Duhe family had just decided not to be sued, which, so far, the other defendants and the court ignored.

The request for an extension of time in itself was not unusual, and courts often grant such motions if the delay wouldn't cause any significant harm. What was unusual about the motion was that it was filed jointly by four of the five defendants. Here, in a case alleging the defendants were guilty of a conspiracy, the parties admitted they would be acting in concert.

I imagined Chevron telling the families, "You dopes, keep your mouths shut. We're taking over now!"

I wondered whether the joint motion was an admission of guilt. If Chevron and Texaco were innocent of what the lawsuit alleged, they wouldn't have joined with the families who might have done something the oil companies didn't even know about. If they weren't involved in a conspiracy, why would the oil companies defend these families? When I told my son Ray-Ray about the joint filing, he didn't miss the irony. He chuckled and said, "That sounds like some RICO stuff."[40]

I felt relieved and proud. I finally felt I was being represented by a skillful, honest attorney. But then something happened. Kim got a text and a phone call from Gabe. He asked her for $7,000 to pay for another abstract that would analyze the ownership and use of the land. Gabe said he'd hired a consultant to do this work and he didn't want to pay for it. Kim told him she was surprised he would incur litigation costs without my approval and he should be talking to me about this. He said he was just making sure the Carrier's abstract was correct and apparently it was. We didn't need another abstract, certainly not for the appeals process. Kim told Gabe she wouldn't pay him. He told Kim he'd talk to me about it and then sent the abstract documents to Kim. But he never told me about them or sent me the documents.

35

THE PANDEMIC

THE YEAR 2020 WAS LIKE something out of a horror movie for my family and my community. Early that year, my oldest son, Ray-Ray, was diagnosed with an aggressive form of lymphoma. He was going through chemotherapy and needed a bone marrow transplant after that. He was diagnosed just before he was ready to open a powerwash company. He'd bought the equipment and the signs and the company t-shirts. Everything was waiting now, stored in our backyard. The pandemic, and Ray's diagnosis changed so many things for him, and the four children he was raising as a single parent. His oldest son who was attending college on a football scholarship in North Louisiana transferred to a school closer to his dad. His daughter who was attending nursing school decided to put off her studies so she could earn money as a travel nurse and relieve her dad of some of the stress in his life.

It's hard to explain the feelings I had about my strong, loving son having such a terrible illness. I knew he would have to go through horrible medical procedures to survive. His condition was probably a result of the the poisons he had been exposed to while serving in the USArmy in Kosovo, where he was transporting depleted uranium, and was exposed to gas fumes and burn pits I was so proud of him for serving his country and grateful he'd come back alive from that war. Now he would have to fight for his life again.

So there was the stress and uncertainty of all that when the COVID-19 pandemic exploded a few months later. The pandemic hit the West End hard. We lost hundreds of residents, mostly the elderly, some living in nursing homes and people who were "essential workers."

West End residents were disproportionately affected by the pandemic because it was hard for a lot of us to quarantine. Families lived in small homes. If people didn't work, they couldn't feed their families. The federal government sent out Covid relief checks but a lot of people in the West End didn't qualify because their incomes were too low to file taxes or they were elderly dependents of their children. A lot of people couldn't even draw unemployment because they were between jobs. I couldn't find any of our local Black-owned businesses who got payments from the federal Paycheck Protection Program (PPP) money, although I found a document that showed a lot of PPP funds went to a lot of the white-owned businesses in town. The local banks made those funding decisions. Some in the West End believed the banks weren't interested in helping the businesses on our side of town.

The City wasn't helping us either. There were Covid testing sites on the other side of the bayou, but so many people in the West End didn't have cars. It took months of asking to get a testing site in the West End. All we got that year was a mobile unit for one day in June.

At first, we didn't have masks either. Fruit of the Loom sent thousands to the city for distribution to the community, but I heard from someone at City Hall that the city council members put them away in a storage room. Several of us made a fuss and the City finally distributed the masks to the community, but there weren't nearly enough.

So the West End was left to its own damn bootstraps again. A friend I and I made hundreds of masks because there just weren't enough to go around. We got donations of Japanese batik and African mud cloth and quilting cotton. For the kids, we had prints of princesses and footballs. We enjoyed working together on this. We sold some of the masks and gave a lot of them away.

Fortunately, we got help from outside. Second Harvest, a large nonprofit organization, donated food from time to time. In October, they delivered 100,000 pounds of produce, meat and dairy to West End Park. They brought individual boxes that included apples, potatoes, roasting chickens, carrots, milk, and big blocks of cheese. The cars were lined up for several blocks on Obie Street hours before the distribution was scheduled to begin at 11:00. People without cars came too, some on bikes, others pushing supermarket carts or baby strollers. Volunteers delivered some of the boxes to low-income housing projects and families living in mobile homes who didn't have a way to haul the boxes home.

Our neighborhood association was managing things and we had lots of volunteers, including several members of the City Council, so the day felt like a community event. (Mayor DeCourt didn't show up for the food distribution, but that week he did celebrate the re-opening of the local McDonald's with a posting on his Facebook page.)

But that food distribution also showed how bad things were in the community. We were used to having lots of people show up for the food distributions. But that fall, the numbers of people who showed up were much bigger than in the past. It was different too, because it was the first time white residents came for food. We knew many of them were uncomfortable. As someone told me, "We know how to get down there and peck with the chickens," but the white folks weren't used to this. I knew they didn't like thinking that Blacks were helping them, and most of the volunteers that day were Black. But we never judged anyone and everyone was especially respectful. No one waits in line for food for two hours who isn't in need. I think that day resulted in a little mutual understanding.

The pandemic was hard on my momma. Before the pandemic, she had a routine that kept her going. A van would pick her up every morning and take her to the day center where she would be with her friends for most of the day. They'd socialize and go to zydeco dancing, bingo games, or the casino. Sometimes they'd have picnics in the park or play games. All of that kept her mentally healthy. But when the pandemic came, the day center closed to protect their clients from Covid. Momma had to stay home all day and missed seeing her friends. We knew if she ever went back, some of her friends wouldn't be there. So many of them were dying from Covid.

My family was struggling a lot that year, living on so little income. I acted calm, but I prayed a lot and worried a lot. I felt I couldn't give in to my anxieties because so much was depending on me. My family needed me to be healthy. When the bills arrived, I just left them unopened until I could pay them.

I got a little relief from the stress by cooking. I remembered an avocado sandwich Kim made for me once when she was in town visiting. It was so healthy and delicious with cheese and mustard and Killer Dave's bread. "It's just an avocado sandwich," she said, but to me it was special because it wasn't the kind of food you'd normally find in New Iberia. So I called her where she was staying in California and asked her to share some healthy recipes. She loved the idea. Every week or two, she'd have a box of groceries delivered from Rouse's or the Super 1, and we'd cook together on a zoom call or over the phone. I made things like eggplant parmesan and roasted vegetables, big salads, and soups full of vegetables. My body felt happier and the family loved what I was making. One evening, my 10-year-old grandson, Dorian, came for dinner. He looked at what was on the table and said "MawMaw, that's white people food!"

That summer, we watched Black Lives Matter demonstrations and speeches on the TV, advocating against police brutality and the murders of young Black men. White people were standing up for the rights of the rest of us. At first, this gave us a little bit of hope because things weren't getting better when Trump was in office. Confederate flags were flying across the bayou and even on signs right in the middle of downtown. The older people said it reminded them of the fears they felt during Jim Crow.

The demonstrations started a lot of conversations about how to make our world more just and less violent. I guess somewhere inside us, we all knew this would trigger a reaction in New Iberia. While the demonstrations were still going on all over the country, a white coalition in New Iberia organized a huge Trump parade. The parade went up and down Admiral Doyle Street, with white men waving flags and stirring up people's fears. Black residents didn't have a parade or a demonstration. We knew if we did, the police would be haranguing us and trying to track down the people who were a part of it. And I guess the majority in Iberia Parish preferred things that way because, a couple of years later, the leader of the coalition that organized that parade was elected to the Louisiana State Senate.

New Iberia's mayor, Freddie DeCourt, made some comments about Black Lives Matter at a city council meeting around that time. Mayor DeCourt was the same mayor who owned the Bayou Teche Trading Company that had been remodeled just before Phanat opened it as NILA Gallery. He was the same mayor who told me it wasn't his fault that the City closed down the West End's pool around the same time he proposed the City build a second pool in a white neighborhood.

"The good thing is we live in New Iberia," he said, "and we have a long history of tolerance, of working together, of being a community. We are that kind of a culture." We never were that kind of culture.

36

MASTER PLAN

The pandemic created delays in the court system and we weren't expecting quick action on the appeal. As if the pandemic wasn't trouble enough, in September, Hurricane Laura came through southwest Louisiana and caused a lot of damage. The worst of it was in Lake Charles, where the 3rd Circuit's courthouse was located. The defendants' reply briefs were due the day before the hurricane was expected to hit land, but the court system was shut down that day for the weather. We didn't know when the reply briefs would be filed.

Meanwhile, the City's neglect of the West End continued. After hearing for years that the City couldn't afford to provide services in the West End, Mayor DeCourt proposed a Master Plan that would allocate millions of dollars to projects for the benefit other parts of the city.[41] West End residents only learned about the proposal by accident because the announcement only made it as far as the town's newspaper. Not many West End residents read the *Daily Iberian* because of how rarely it reported on anything of interest to us.

The article in the *Daily Iberian* about the mayor's Master Plan said the mayor wanted residents to weigh in on a long list of proposed projects to revitalize the community. It quoted the mayor as saying, "What I'm trying to do is pull a bunch of groups together" to understand what residents wanted. I was surprised at this. Earlier in the year, the mayor had promised our neighborhood association a place at the table for this planning process. When it finally got going, the mayor didn't inform me or any of our neighborhood associations board members. I didn't know of anyone in the West End who had been asked to participate in the plan, including Phanat, but I knew of a lot of people on the other side of town who had.

In other ways, the mayor's process for how to spend a lot of money seemed designed to stifle community participation. The Master Plan proposal wasn't at New Iberia's website, or available to the "bunch of groups" the mayor said he was pulling together. City Council meeting minutes didn't refer to the Master Plan either. Some of us asked for copies of the proposal and a way to participate. The mayor's office told us the only way to see the proposed Master Plan was to schedule a "tour" of the proposal in Mayor DeCourt's very own private building off of Main Street. The same one that had once been NILA Gallery, which had once been run by Phanat's nonprofit and then became the mayor's private party venue called Bayou Teche Trading Company. The Bayou Teche Trading Company's logo was included on the materials advertising the "tours."

I couldn't go to one of the tours because I was careful about being in closed rooms. I didn't want to expose my family to Covid, especially my momma. And really, I just couldn't trust myself to be polite about what was going on. But Kim went to one of these tours where the mayor gave a presentation, maskless, in a small room. Kim told me later that the City had a lot of glitzy-for-New-Iberia posters, maps, and presentation materials at the presentation. She picked up some city documents that included the mayor's business information and logo.

At the meeting, the mayor referred to how the proposed projects would improve residents' quality of life. He wanted the City to build pocket parks, a boat dock, a kayak dock and a new bandstand. He was going to update the signage, remodel the pool house in City Park, close the public bathrooms used by the homeless, and remove large planter boxes to increase parking on Main Street.

The mayor's plan also proposed to build a new pool near Admiral Doyle Drive in a neighborhood where well-heeled white residents sent their children to a Catholic school. This felt personal. He didn't have the money to give us back the pool that was paved over when he was a council member. When I asked him about this, he explained that it wasn't his decision to pave over the pool in the West End. But now, he was going to find a way to build another pool in a neighborhood far from where West End kids were living.

Mayor DeCourt's vision didn't seem to take into account any of the West End's needs or priorities. For our part of town, he proposed a dog park, even though few West End residents owned dogs. He proposed a pickleball court, even though residents in the West End didn't play pickleball. He proposed more destruction of abandoned houses rather than their revitalization. He proposed an African American Museum but said the City didn't have any money for it. He explained his expectation that a local historian could raise funds for it.

The mayor's Master Plan didn't propose to reinstate programs or facilities in the West End — its swimming pool, the children's summer camp, the library, or the youth recreation programs. It didn't propose any public transportation or support for local businesses. It didn't propose ways to create jobs or teach job skills to reduce the drug trafficking and violence. Instead, the Master Plan suggested the West End address crime by relying on "partnerships" between nonprofits, churches, and the police. The mayor said there wasn't money in the budget for that. We'd have to find the funding ourselves. I doubted the people of the West End would agree to partnerships with the local police after years of harassment and surveillance. As for the churches, most of them had all but abandoned work as community-builders.

At the meeting, the mayor explained that the projects in his Master Plan would attract tourism. Maybe the mayor didn't know that economists were predicting a grim future for tourism because of the pandemic. I'd never been much of a tourist, but I knew what tourists wanted wasn't new signage or pocket parks. New Iberia didn't have much to offer tourists besides middle-brow chain hotels, mediocre restaurants, and the Shadows on the Teche, a plantation that wasn't much different from the plantations all over Louisiana.

I was troubled by the mayor's proposals, but not surprised. As usual, our city government was looking out for downtown and the white neighborhoods, and advising the West End to get services from nonprofits and the police. It always seemed like a secret that the City's grant money and the savings from eliminating West End services would be used to improve other neighborhoods. But now it wasn't a secret. Taking money from the West End and using it in other neighborhoods was right out in the open.

The City wanted to build something new that looks nice on the outside, but if you don't clean up the old, the new is built on injustice and other people's pain. You can't pretend it's good here by putting a Band-Aid on it. It's still lies inside. One of the lies was what happened to my family's land. The ways the City treated the West End and the ways the legal system treated my family were all part of one bigger lie.

37

THE DECISION ON APPEAL

On the day of the 2020 election, we got some shocking news. The body of 15-year-old Quanam "Bobby" Charles was found face down in the mud of a sugarcane field not far from the Carrier land. Bobby's parents had reported him missing three days before, but local police suggested they check the local football game. We don't know how but the Iberia Parish Sheriff's Department found the body. It waited more than 12 hours to tell the family, and didn't alert local media. At first, the Iberia Parish Sheriff's Department called the death a drowning. But photos of the body showed that Bobby had been beaten. The last time Bobby was seen was with a white woman named Janet Irvin, and her teenage son. Irvin didn't come forward with that information until another child reported it to local police.[42]

A few days later, Irvin left town. The local police chief was the son of Glen Romero, the one who was farming sugarcane on the Carrier land. After a public outcry, Irvin was arrested several months later on charges of contributing to the delinquency of a minor. But we never learned what happened to Bobby.[43]

These kinds of crimes in New Iberia were rarely solved and we all knew that if Bobby had been white, local law enforcement would treat the case differently. Our country was still investigating and reporting on the 1996 murder of JonBenet Ramsey, but no one in power seemed to care about Bobby's murder any more, even in his own home town. I heard a white resident of New Iberia speak at a public meeting, blaming the crime rate in New Iberia on "them" across the bayou. Afterwards, I asked him who "them" was and why he thought New Iberia's crime problem was only in my part of town. The white community had its share of domestic violence, sexual assaults, and shootings. I invited him to a public discussion of this. I never heard back from him.

While the people of the West End were begging for justice for Bobby, I got the news I that I wouldn't be getting justice for my family. On November 12, 2020, the appellate court affirmed the lower court's decision.[44] The decision didn't deny the claims of our lawsuit, just as the evidence didn't and the lower court hadn't. It just said my family had waited too long to file the lawsuit. It didn't rule on all of our procedural claims or permit us to reopen the case to show why the theory of "prescription" shouldn't apply in this case. The decision seemed to leave open the possibility of continued, more limited, litigation but reading it on my own, it wasn't clear about exactly what that might mean.

I couldn't talk about the appellate court's decision for weeks. It followed me around all day long like a bad dream. There were so many 'if only's'. If only Floyd could have filed the lawsuit 15 years before. If only I'd been able to file the lawsuit with another lawyer after Floyd's conviction. If only Karen hadn't hired oil and gas lawyers in Texas. If only Karen had filed the lawsuit as soon as she became administrator, If only my family could have filed a lawsuit at any time during the previous 80 years.

After I was able to face it, Gabe didn't seem interested in talking. I contacted him several times before he responded. He didn't say much about the decision. He said he wanted to visit the land. He didn't say why and he'd never asked before, but we agreed to meet there on December 19, 2020.

We met at the gas station on Old Jeanerette Road, close to the property. I got out of my car and got into his. I directed him to the dirt road adjacent to the land. At the wooden gate, Gabe stopped and got out of the car. He looked at something written on the gate. He didn't say what he was looking at or looking for, and we kept driving to the site of the pumpjack. It was still squeaking and grinding, pumping oil out of the ground on Carrier land. We walked around the land. Gabe said the placement of a fire extinguisher 50 feet from a small outbuilding suggested some kind of special hazard.

Then he called his legal associate, Casey, who had helped write our appeal to the court. Gabe was on speakerphone with her and I could hear their conversation. He gave her the exact location of the pumping oil well. After a couple of minutes, she told him there wasn't supposed to be anything there.

"I'm here now and I'm looking at it," he said, or something like that. Casey told him she'd just checked the State's website and there were no records to show a registered oil well at the site. Gabe said the drilling was operating illegally whether or not the Carriers had authorized it.

On that same day, Gabe contacted Kim. Gabe knew I trusted Kim and she was following the lawsuit, but she wasn't his client and he shouldn't have been talking to her or anyone else about my family's lawsuit without my permission, She told me later Gabe said he had some concerns about the configuration of the land; that he had some doubts about whether the land belonged to the Carriers. He wondered why the house that burned down in the 1950s was so far from the drilling rig. Kim told him that virtually everyone involved had conceded that the land belonged to the Carriers. She told him the royalties contract between Chevron and Karen's mother, Shirley May, was evidence that Chevron knew the Carriers owned the land. Kim asked Gabe why he'd never raised this before with me, and why he was talking to her about it instead of me. Gabe said something was "suspicious," and he'd get back to her after he did some research. He never got back to her, and he never talked to me about it either. That was something suspicious.

After the visit to the land, Gabe didn't respond to my many texts and emails for almost two months. He knew I wanted to meet with him about the next steps in the lawsuit. I didn't understand all the procedural requirements, and I was worried we'd miss a deadline.

In early February 2021, I saw a Facebook posting by the court clerk, Iberia Parish's Court Clerk. The same court clerk who wrote the letter to the appellate court explaining that he couldn't give the court a certified copy of the transcript. The Facebook posting showed the court clerk swearing in Gabe as the city attorney of Delcambre on February 8, 2021. Gabe didn't tell me about this even though I was still his client and he knew I was hoping to continue the litigation. His new job arguably created a conflict of interest because he'd be representing a city in the same parish where my family was suing the parish's District Attorney and where parish judges were deciding my family's case.

I waited a couple of days before I sent him a text congratulating him on his appointment. He immediately responded not with a "thank you," but by asking me, "Is that published somewhere LOL?" I sent him a screenshot of the photo from the court clerk's Facebook post. After that, Gabe didn't respond to my texts or phone call messages for three more months. In May, he finally agreed to meet with me.

We didn't have a lot of time left to pursue some of the legal actions that were remaining to us. At our May 2021 meeting, Gabe reiterated our legal options, and apologized for his delay in getting back to me. He asked me whether I had a copy of the 1916 pooling agreement. Right there, I sent it to him on email, and he printed it out. As we were leaving, Gabe said he'd let me know about what he thought we should do. For weeks after that, I sent Gabe numerous texts asking for information about the status of my family's case. He never responded.

Although Gabe didn't talk to me again about my family's case, he did respond to a reporter. She was working on a podcast about the health effects of stress and was interested in my family's litigation. The reporter and I went to Gabe's office for a meeting the two of them set up. When Gabe saw us, he was rude and agitated, asking me why we were meeting with the reporter. "What's this all about anyway?" We left his office. I was shaken by how rudely and disrespectfully he'd spoken to me, especially in front of a reporter.

A few days later, Gabe met with the reporter alone. He didn't tell me about the meeting, but the reporter later told Kim about her conversation with Gabe. She said it lasted for over two hours, that Gabe was charming and talked at length about my family's lawsuit. He told her my family didn't really have a case. She told Kim that Gabe referred to a land map that showed the location of the oil facilities were not on my family's land. The only map that showed this was the map that had been tampered with in the 1950s, which Gabe knew had been falsified. He also knew that every other piece of evidence confirmed the very facts he had presented to the court in our appeal. The reporter aired her podcast a couple of months later. It included information that might raise doubts about the evidence in my family's case. I had never given Gabe permission to speak privately to a reporter about my case and he never told me what he said to her.

After hearing the podcast, Kim sent Gabe a text to let him know that, in California at least, a lawyer could be disbarred for disclosing confidential information about a client's lawsuit to a reporter. She didn't hear back from him.

I didn't either. It took me a long time to face the thought that Gabe betrayed me. Looking back, I wonder whether he was ever truly my advocate because of the critical times he ignored my messages, and talked to people about my case without my permission. He never followed up on the legal actions he said were remaining to us. In 2024, I engaged a fifth lawyer to help me get an accounting from him and the return of my family's case files.

In September 2022, Keith Mayo was disbarred from practicing law in the State of Texas for failing to represent the interests of his client.[45] The court ordered Mayo to return case files to all of his clients and former clients. Mayo never sent the Carrier files to me or my family. Maybe he sent them to Gabe. I'll probably never know.

38

WHERE THINGS STAND

IT'S BEEN A COUPLE OF years since the court issued the appellate decision in my family's lawsuit. A lot has happened since then, some of it painful and some of it hopeful.

Momma passed in October 2021. She was 84. In those last years, Momma had slowed down a lot, and wasn't able to do all the things she most loved to do. She'd always been a strong independent person, but in those last days, she didn't mind depending on me. I loved every minute caring for her and loving on her. She was my mother, my hero, my Siamese twin.

Then my big brother Marcus passed in 2022. He was only 63. I miss him terribly.

I'm trying to feel hopeful about the city government of New Iberia. There is still a lot of neglect and pretending that the West End is getting its fair share. I don't think much is going to change in my lifetime, but some good things have happened too. The plantation in town, the Shadows on the Teche, has recently begun to acknowledge the enslavement of most of the people who once lived there. It's a very small part of the story of New Iberia, but it helps. The City didn't install a pickleball court or a dog park in the West End, which we didn't need, but it renovated our Community Center, which we desperately needed. After completing the work, the City co-hosted a dinner dance there called "Celebrating Black Excellence." The event was a big success and the community is making plans to do it again. Phanat is moving back into town and posted on Facebook that he's thinking about getting Envision Da Berry going again.

Our neighborhood association got some private funding to do a lot more home repairs and disaster relief, so we have been doing a lot of work in the community, like ramps for the disabled and replacing hazardous heating systems. One of our recent projects involved replacing a roof and a disabled ramp for Miss Amanda, the mother of two autistic children who had to use crutches. Before the repairs, the house inside was littered with buckets to catch the rainwater coming in through the ceiling, and the children had to be lifted outside through a window because the porch was so rotten. Now they can stay dry all year and walk out the front door and down the porch steps on their own.

My family is doing well. Our hardest challenges are behind us for now. Ray-Ray got strong enough to be up and about. He'll have to manage his cancer for the rest of his life, but he's making the best of it. After Ray-Ray finished his treatments, his daughter Kyrell went back to nursing school and she's working as a registered nurse now in Lake Charles.

All of the grandchildren are good students and good people. Two of my grandsons, Terrelle and Latrelle, are attending the University of Louisiana in Lafayette. Dorian attends a school for gifted students because of his musical talents, and Carter recently sold his first painting. Latrelle became a father last year, so I'm a great-grandma to a little boy named Landon. We have his toys and baby equipment covering the living room floor, so we're always ready for him to visit. Ray painted the house last year and seems happy to be retired. He's not pushing me on a swing any more, but he is the best companion I could have. All of this is almost more than I could hope for, to have my family thriving and close.

Last year, I started working with veterans, helping them understand the services they qualify for, like health care and educational opportunities. I have an office in Lafayette, and I can work at home some of the time. Because I know the armed services and I loved serving my country, I understand something about how my clients feel. They open up to me about their anxieties and struggles. This work gives me one more reason to get up in the morning.

For now at least, the lawsuit is behind me. I don't know where I'd find a lawyer to represent my family and I don't know whether I have the strength in me to start up all over again. It didn't work out the way I'd hoped, but I did the best I could and I got as far down the road as I could. I don't think I failed. I think the system failed me. It failed Fay, who was with me in the courthouse files and the land office in Baton Rouge, up early mornings on the phone to share ideas. Like so many others in my family, Fay left us before she could see how her work changed things.

No one knows what will happen in the years to come, but I don't think this is an ending. Maybe it's a beginning for my children and my grandchildren and now my great-grandchild. I owed them the story of their ancestors and a place on the path to justice. Some of them will move on from the kind of pain their family and community have lived with for generations. Some will find meaning in feeding the hungry, like my daddy did. Some will stay and fight, like my momma did. Whatever they do, they all need to know this is the way of our world: that fairness and justice are never sure, that good people can be compromised by a bad system, and that we can only find meaning in our lives by our commitment to what is best in us.

I know my family is not alone in this. I know my own neighbors are suffering from hundreds of years of cruelty that no amount of courage could change. They wake every day knowing they don't have the power to claim what belongs to them, and wake in the middle of the night afraid of what more their children could lose. Not just land or wealth, but dignity and fairness and freedom from fear.

I lost a lawsuit because of betrayals and a misuse of our government. But I won a little bit of freedom because I can tell my ancestors that they are acknowledged, that they can lie in peace, and their lives were worth more than what others did to them.

And I know my assignment wasn't to win a lawsuit. It was finding the truth and telling it. And I did that.

ACKNOWLEDGMENTS

WE ARE SO GRATEFUL FOR the support of friends and family who encouraged our efforts to tell the Carrier family's story. We thank those who provided essential insights and edits on drafts of this memoir, including Laura Malcolm Olzman, Dr. Karen Sokal, Janet Econome, Vic Weisser, Catherine Marenghi, Bonnie Lee Black, Susan Brown, Ann Black, and Jodi Pincus. We also thank Carole Schor for her expert copy editing and Mary Meade for book design and technical assistance.

Mostly we want to express our love for the people of New Iberia and all people who, with generations of their families, have struggled with the indignities and injustice of racism.

ENDNOTES

1. https://theind.com/articles/12451/
2. I found the records of these transactions and proceedings in Opelousas in the St. Landry Parish court files. They were there because a Catholic priest named Father Hebert kept track of the official records of Blacks in the area at a time when the courts didn't.
3. Today, not many Black families own farm land. Between 1910 and 2007, Black farm owners as a group lost 80% of their land. The USDA, in particular, has become notorious for its disparate treatment of Black farmers in providing loans and credit for farming operations, knowing the land would be sold to white farmers in a fire sale. https://www.naacpldf.org/case-issue/black-farmers-faq/
https://www.Mommajones.com/food/2021/04/Black-land-matters-farmers-justice-leah-penniman-fannie-lou-hamer-cory-booker-land-tenure/
https://www.americanprogress.org/issues/

economy/reports/2019/04/03/467892/progressive-governance-can-turn-tide-Black-farmers/ https://features.propublica.org/Black-land-loss/heirs-property-rights-why-Black-families-lose-land-south
4. Little Bayou is also called "Ti" Bayou, short for the French word, "petit," meaning little.
5. A lot of Louisiana's oil history is recounted in HydroCarbon Hucksters: Lessons from Louisiana on Oil, Politics, and Environmental Justice, Ernest Zebrowski and Mariah Zebrowski Leach. University Press of Mississippi, 2014.
6. See HydroCarbon Hucksters: *Lessons from Louisiana on Oil, Politics, and Environmental Justice,* Ernest Zebrowski and Mariah Zebrowski Leach. University Press of Mississippi, 2014.
7. Because Blacks didn't have access to the recordkeeping of the parish court system, the churches often served that function, as did that Baptist church.
8. https://web.archive.org/web/20190914003857/http://www.losapos.com/lakepeigneur
9. https://www.upi.com/Archives/1983/07/07/Settlement-reached-in-Jeff-Island-accident/4485426398400/
10. https://www.cntraveler.com/stories/2016-07-11/how-louisianas-lake-peigneur-became-200-feet-

deep-in-an-instant
https://www.iberianet.com/news/lake-peigneur-bubbling-persists/article_68c738d9-ebb4-51ff-abc8-9b4771f16d17.html
https://curioushistorian.com/lake-peigneur-and-the-diamond-crystal-salt-mine-disaster

11. The City of New Iberia and a map of it is described in this article. https://storymaps.arcgis.com/stories/721eb86ddc6a4c499dbaf6f5e51e6ef3

12. During World War II, a handful of local Black leaders applied for federal funds to build a welding school in response to President Roosevelt's Executive Order 8802. The order prohibited racial discrimination in companies with contracts to support the war effort.
http://docs.fdrlibrary.marist.edu/odex8802.html
The federal government approved the grant to build the welding school in New Iberia and the school opened in May 1944. The school raised hopes for self-reliance and skilled jobs for West End residents. A week after the school opened, the parish Sheriff, Gilbert Ozenne, and his deputies beat, threatened and drove out of town the school's organizers, as well as most of the town's Black professionals, among them doctors, teachers, and an insurance agent. The welding school shut down shortly after.

13. In 1755, the English Governor of Canada ordered French-speaking citizens of "Acadie" in Nova Scotia to swear allegiance to the British Crown. If they didn't, they would be exiled. Many refused and migrated to southwest Louisiana.
14. What some residents call the city's "bible," *New Iberia: Its History and People* was 507 pages long, mostly memorializing hundreds of years of white residents' achievements, festivals, local businesses, war heroes, and farming. The only chapter about Black history is 23-pages, presents polite descriptions of churches, schools, and small businesses. It omits any accounts of slavery, Jim Crow, civil rights, or the many achievements of New Iberia's Blacks. The book was published by the University of Louisiana Press and, as of January 2024, was still available at the campus bookstore in Lafayette.
https://books.google.com.mx/books?id=LVwEAAAAMBAJ&pg=PA25&lpg=PA25&dq=Frenzella+Volter&source=bl&ots=K4nNNrsHw_&sig=ACfU3U0-ph4Zg59Uf7erAYmVrSThB0QS0Q&hl=en&sa=X&redir_esc=y#v=onepage&q=Frenzella%20Volter&f=false
15. By 2023 and after years of wrangling by a few knowledgeable residents, the Bayou Teche Museum introduced some references to the City's Black

community and history.
16. https://www.freddiedecourt.com/political-involvement.html
17. http://theind.com/article-12451-the-ugly-secret-at-little-bayou.html
18. https://www.iberianet.com/news/armenco-project-moves-ahead/article_f62db826-7e4c-11e5-a2e7-c75fe6d271f9.html
19. https://www.iberianet.com/news/west-end-rising-work-begins-on-final-home-damaged-by/article_d5d98806-c2a2-11e7-a492-973c893c7bfc.html
20. https://www.iberianet.com/news/new-iberia-is-magazine-s-city-of-the-year/article_0d0b74b8-b3b4-11e7-bf11-ebc8c86316ff.html
21. https://www.theadvocate.com/acadiana/news/crime_police/article_a6cd5330-ef56-11e8-969b-b361f1b7e760.html
22. https://theind.com/articles/6689/
23. https://theind.com/articles/12451/
24. https://www.theadvocate.com/acadiana/news/crime_police/article_7637a812-ec16-11e8-b82f-9b135d793f43.html
25. https://www.usnews.com/news/best-states/Louisiana/articles/2017-03-28/7-ex-sheriffs-deputies-sentenced-to-prison-in-beatings-case
https://www.nytimes.com/2017/02/08/magazine/the-preacher-and-the-sheriff.html

https://www.nola.com/news/courts/records-325k-settlement-paid-in-death-of-victor-white-iii-in-iberia-parish-sheriffs-patrol/article_db11cec8-90c7-11ea-8946-77f880153e63.html

26. https://www.citylab.com/equity/2019/07/iberia-parish-sheriff-Louisiana-Alphonse-ackal-election/593839/ https://Louisianavoice.com/2018/07/16/more-than-6m-paid-out-by-sheriffs-offices-in-judgments-settlements-since-2015-attorney-fees-add-another-1-4m/

27. https://www.census.gov/quickfacts/iberiaparishLouisiana https://www.iberianet.com/news/ipso-has-settled-3-5m-worth-of-lawsuits-since-jan-2018/article_73f535ce-3f0e-11e9-8758-07499e9c21f3.html https://theappeal.org/an-infamous-Louisiana-sheriff-is-on-his-way-out-now-what/

28. https://envision-da-berry-2.square.site/

29. https://www.techegrowers.org/

30. The Carrier pooling agreement also listed other Black families with land on the salt dome. I don't know whether they were real or fictitious. I couldn't find any records that they owned the land or ever got any royalties according to the terms of the pooling agreement. The land was being farmed in sugarcane.

31. For years, local residents petitioned parish officials to remove the mural. Courthouse officials replied they would work on it. Finally in 2021, the parish covered the mural with a curtain.
https://www.iberianet.com/news/courtroom-mural-under-fire-for-apparent-racist-overtones/article_557de616-b5d4-11ea-861e-ff923d6c43be.html
http://www.courthouses.co/us-states/h-l/louisiana/iberia-parish/
32. https://www.iberianet.com/breaking_news/thibodeaux-sentenced-to-months/article_a34c3106-b312-11e9-b613-ab58e89f08d6.html
https://www.iberianet.com/elections/ditch-elected-clerk-of-court-with-percent-of-vote-in/article_e6e79bba-ed89-11e9-9e8d-972738f1197a.html
33. https://www.theadvocate.com/acadiana/news/courts/article_0eb4059e-fc11-11e9-ba8b-f7a90d3cef3d.html
34. https://www.theadvocate.com/acadiana/news/courts/article_a05d3dda-1d2c-11ea-bda5-1b609c5eb5f6.html
35. This is Kim's blog posting found in Wilson's files. https://kimmie53.com/2019/03/02/louisiana-noire/#more-11510
36. The use of the term here means the heirs to the property.

37. Kim loaned me the money with funds from her aunt's estate.
38. In American common law, there is a tort called "slander of title," a claim when "an entity publishes a false statement that disparages or clouds another entity's title to property," https://en.wikipedia.org/wiki/Slander_of_title
39. https://louisianavoice.com/2018/07/05/the-political-pot-in-iberia-parish-just-continues-boiling-with-more-reports-of-retaliatory-actions-by-local-elected-officials/
40. RICO stands for "Racketeer-Influenced and Corrupt Organizations and refers to federal law addressing organized crime. https://www.justice.gov/jm/jm-9-110000-organized-crime-and-racketeering
41. The use of "master" has been fading from use because of its association with slavery. Calling an official city document a "master plan" seemed ironically appropriate in New Iberia, especially given its intent to focus spending in white neighborhoods. https://www.csmonitor.com/The-Culture/In-a-Word/2021/0628/As-English-evolves-so-too-does-the-word-master
42. https://www.nytimes.com/2021/02/11/us/janet-irvin-quawan-bobby-charles.html

43. https://www.cbsnews.com/news/quawan-bobby-charles-found-dead-janet-irwin-charges-louisiana/
44. The judge who wrote it had once sat on the Iberia Parish Court, and was known to be friends with two of the defendants' families.
45. https://www.texasbar.com/AM/Template.cfm?Section=Find_A_Lawyer&template=/Customsource/MemberDirectory/Sanction.cfm&JWID=6077646

www.ingramcontent.com/pod-product-compliance
Lightning Source LLC
Chambersburg PA
CBHW070730020526
44118CB00035B/1160